Civic Garden Centre
Library

FLOWERS:
FREE FORM – INTERPRETIVE DESIGN

FLOWERS:

FREE FORM—

INTERPRETIVE

DESIGN

M. BENZ, *Bachelor of Science*

SAN JACINTO PUBLISHING COMPANY

P. O. BOX 6254   HOUSTON 6, TEXAS

III

First printing—May 1960
Library of Congress No. 59-15356

Copyright 1960©
San Jacinto Publishing Co.
P. O. Box 6254 • Houston, Texas

Printed in the United States of America

FULL PAGE COLOR PLATES BY JIM THOMAS

OTHER PHOTOGRAPHS BY BESSIE HINTON EIDSON AND M. BENZ

V

Flowers are the manifestation of God's love
for his people. They are
the hieroglyphics of diety.

Flowers are the only material things given
to man by which he expresses his
most vital relationships of faith in
immortality, of hope, and of love
for his fellow man.

Only flowers can express his
deepest emotion.

Flowers speak for man.

THE AUTHOR

Foreword

A new concept has evolved from the floral art of the past. Contemporary trends and pure form, using basic principles of design, are forging into prominence. Freedom of expression currently evolving in floral art is indicative of the contemporary changes in other art forms such as painting, sculpture, and architecture. This modern trend is toward less conformity to fashion and tradition, simplification of materials, presentation, and the yielding to international influences. Art changes, along with scientific advances, are producing a totally new culture. In any transition, much that is extreme and bizarre always appears, but inevitably there emerge from the experimental stages excellent examples of stable new art forms. The author's designing is compatible with present day thinking, interior decor, architecture, and education. The designs in this book, showing a new beauty, freshness and vigor, speak for themselves. They justify this freedom. True creative ability finds infinite expression without being encumbered by rules and limitations. *Design assumes a new, clear meaning.*

I dedicate this book—

To those who share my love of flowers.

" 'Tis better to give a flower
than a jewel. Thou canst not
help but weigh the price of the
jewel to value the gift; but a
flower brings true sentiment
shorn of all but love."

FROM FLOWERS: THEIR CREATIVE DESIGN

Also by M. Benz—FLOWERS: Their Creative Designs

What authorities are saying about—
   FLOWERS: Their Creative Designs

"The finest book ever published in this field."
"Here is a book that is literally worth its weight in gold. . . . It is one of the most constructive contributions to the florists' industry in my thirty years in this field."

Willard Crain, Past President,
Florists' Telegraph Delivery Association
National Authority and Commentator

"The inspirational impetus provided in this book, and the practical techniques set forth, make it invaluable reading for all who wish to find a way to wider horizons in floral design in their business and homes."

"This book is highly informative, educational, and would be of invaluable assistance to the experienced and inexperienced, to the professional as well as the amateur."

John Henry Dudley, President
Society of American Florists

"A masterpiece of floral knowledge."
". . . it covers all problems of flower arranging which a florist or garden club member could possibly encounter . . . it is worth its price and we recommend it highly."

The Federated Garden Clubs
of New York State, Inc.

Table of Contents

Pen and Ink Illustrations

"Love of beauty is taste—
The creation of beauty is art."

RALPH WALDO EMERSON.

XX

Chapter **I.** Introduction

Chapter I

An Introduction to Free Form—Interpretive Design

One of the most self-satisfying of all man's accomplishments is the result of work with his hands. The building of a project or the putting together of something is the culmination of an effort beginning as an idea that must be formulated.

It first begins with desire, or the urge to create, to do something constructive and is developed through sustained effort. Some will find this outlet in literature, sculpture, mechanical devices, or in daily living with such menial tasks as baking a cake, sewing, building a boat, or other activity for a livelihood or hobby. Everyone has the capacity to create — it is an attitude, it is drive toward a goal or an ideal.

"Creativity" is not an exclusive attribute given to just a few as a gift of God. It is an inherent quality common to all people. Everyone is born with an appreciation of the beautiful — it varies as to cultivation and expression. It may be a hidden talent of which we are unaware. For instance, Grandma Moses' record speaks for itself. Failures will come but they are the building blocks for the final product. Too often we envision the finished product which appears mountainous and causes us to rebel; however, by taking the problem step by step we can accomplish the work. There are a great number of famous people who, when first starting, were told they had no aptitude for the profession of their choice; but they did not falter,

PLATE 1
Grecian Horse

The glories of Grecian History are embodied in the stately carriage of this horse. The clean cut, bold definite form is contemporary. This abstract flower arrangement is the perfect tribute to this great piece of art. The Golden allium blossoms reproduce the body lines of the statuette. Lilies, perfect in structural form, are symbolic of the Olympic torch. The bold, textured container is a stylized chalice. Rarely does one find materials that complement each other to such a high degree.

PLATE 1   23

and with determination went on to success. So it is with floral design, first trying basic steps, and then moving on to true creative design as we learn the flexibilities of the materials.

Any art form can be considered a spiritual expression of man's self coming from within — a force that must find expression in some medium. It is more than a technical or mechanical skill with paints, clay, stone, or plant materials. It is a natural inner force stemming from a basic desire for self-expression and freedom. This urge to create forces man into motion. Art (design) is emotion — imagination — vision where form takes shape. It is culminated through a medium in rhythmic harmony. As life is motion similar to a growing plant, so is art — it is motion and must progress. It is evolution in rhythmic form: Static form dies. Floral art must move to unlimited horizons and integrate itself with the times to prevent stagnation.

Design in any form, whether musical composition, poetry, literature, sculpture, painting, or floral art requires emotional urge to create and a deep, sensitive understanding of its principles, used with skill of expression and technique.

This sensitive appreciation for creativeness is best expressed by the Persian poet Moslih Saadi, a Mohammedan sheik who lived about the 13th century, in his quatrain concerning two loaves of bread:

If of thy mortal goods thou art bereft
And from thy slender store two loaves alone to thee are left
Sell one, and with the dole
Buy hyacinths to feed thy soul.

It is the feeding of the Soul that illumines the imagination, creates, and evolves functional form — which results in each civilization leaving its record. The body needs food for sustenance — the mind must have visions — imagination for creativeness.

History becomes real to us by the art of the past. The think-

ing, daily activity, and commerce is revealed by this art, thus giving identifying characteristics to each civilization. Every race is remembered by the art forms (designs) it produces and little else.

On the walls of caves, prehistoric man depicted familiar forms of life as he saw them. These pictures immediately give the impression the artist wished to convey. He used various materials at hand and primitive techniques to express his mental picture. The cave dweller left his record; the Egyptian portrayed events of history on the walls of the tombs propitiating spirits; the Greeks developed architecture and sculpture. The Renaissance and early Far Eastern cultures handed down excellent paintings of floral art.

Over the years each civilization preserved portions of the progress of the preceding one and actively incorporated these advances into its daily living. In leisure time decorative motifs were created which were symbolic of heraldry or nationalism. The spiritual urge for further artistic development brought into use these motifs for decoration only. Human instinct, inherent tastes, and the repetition of basic principles evolved new art forms. New concepts and ways of living varied in style, but art principles that developed through early efforts remained as constant as the materials. The principles of design through which we express the artistic are a part of us all. Although we apply the word "modern" or "contemporary" to the work of today, each generation was "modern" during its time. Artistic expressions based on fundamental design principles as they evolved are as pleasing today as they were hundreds of years ago. Only our tastes, ways of living, and modern techniques have changed.

Early art forms were stylized and set by the public's tastes. In France during the latter part of the 19th century artists began to deviate from tradition and public opinion. Art, particularly painting and sculpture, exhibited a new freedom. "Art for art's sake" was on every tongue. Cubism, surrealism, expressionism, impressionism and other schools came into being.

PLATES 2, 3 AND 4
Symphonic Browns

Color and line move like a symphony of tonal values as a theme in music weaves its pattern. The introduction of a green note in the vase and the one hosta leaf is the major chord (color). The over-all minor chord is definitely stated in the quiet clear color of the exotic Malay ginger flower and accessories. The container shares equally with foliage and flowers. Contrast is important, yet equality of units, when carefully handled, gives importance to each without competition. The artist created the container, a self-sufficient object of art, as a thing of beauty; additional materials are secondary. The development of the floral pictures tends only to accent the work of the artist. Form, in both floral material and container, expresses itself in the element of dominance.

Floral art today has reached a milestone marking its maturity. This art stands at the threshold of the greatest advancement of its history through the introduction of a new trend — *Free Form* — *Interpretive Design*. The principles which guided floral art in the past, and through their continued usage, became set rules. These rules were necessary for growth and expansion, to teach the novice, and to point the way. Moreover, they set a standard of excellence by which to judge artistic quality.

The rapid advances in social sciences, industrial environment, manner of living, and thinking have brought many changes to our way of life: Society is becoming more mature. With this maturity comes the ability to accept, to understand, and to use in daily living, unbridled freedom of thought and expression. This freedom has been responsible for the great developments in floral art. The time is now ready to make one of the greatest strides in floral design — that of *Free Form* — *Interpretive Design*. It is not a matter of being a nonconformist but rather the adherence to good principles and the expression of one's self as an individual. Art is the frank, uncensored expression of the artist. It is the refusal to be limited by the rules set by others, and the acceptance of an unlimited sphere governed only by one's self-expression. This has always been characteristic of the American way of life. America was founded on freedom, and it is this same freedom that is being demanded by all peoples of the world today. Floral art is demanding the same freedom.

What is the thinking behind this new trend in floral art?

First, it is awareness of one's own individuality and freedom to express as he wishes, to say in art form, with floral material, what he feels inwardly. It is the breaking away from tradition and the rules of "set" design of strict geometrical configurations. It is self-expression through freedom of style using new materials — artificial, dried, or painted. This new concept in floral arranging will be used to a greater degree in all schools and shows in the future.

To understand the new design concepts of *Free Form —
Interpretive Design,* we must first realize that because of man's emotional and spiritual response to flowers, floral art is in a category
apart from all other arts.

Of all God's creations, none are more beautiful than flowers.
These close companions to the Soul of man are the only material
objects given to him through which he can express his deepest emo-
tions and most vital relationships — love, hope, faith, gratitude —
indeed, even life and death itself. No other material objects can
express beauty of emotion as tenderly as a flower. Flowers are the
hieroglyphics of diety. They have deep spiritual significance to man
and through them he expresses his concepts of beauty, design, mood,
and individuality.

Appreciation in use of flowers is found in all races from the
beginning of time. People have used flowers in their daily living,
festivities, and religious ceremonials throughout history. No man
lives where flowers do not grow. In Central America the Indians
of Guatemala find expression in the use of orange marigolds when
praying for the Souls in purgatory (Plate 33). The Orient is lavish
with folklore and symbolism of flowers. The lotus blossom, symbol
of purity and eternity, is so closely associated with Buddhism that
at no time is the statue of Buddha seen without this flower. The
Japanese foretell the coming of seasons, holidays, and family events
through floral symbolism. Their reverence for floral meaning is so
highly regarded that an arrangement would never be made with a
flower or other plant material out of season, or placed in a container
not suggestive of its individual habits or region of growth (Plate 9).
The spiritual and symbolic attributes of flowers are so deeply rooted
that Americans are often unaware of the influence on their lives.
Their significance is often taken for granted. Yet mention the Easter
lily, our symbol of faith, and its great religious connotation brings
to the Christian mind the perfection we strive for, the resurrection

of Christ, and the beauty of the service on this morning. Speak of lilies-of-the-valley, orchids, poinsettias, chrysanthemums, or red roses, and each paints a picture of significance. Remove the emotional aspect of flowers, their symbolism, and we become static — mechanical.

Today, for gracious living, flowers are considered a necessity. Floral designers must meet the challenge of fostering and teaching the great joys and satisfactions of floral art. To do this properly we must diligently strive to master design and use it unrestricted in expression.

Floral art is popular because it satisfies the need for creative self-expression. The great wealth of material at hand, in the garden, woodland, and especially the exotic flora from foreign countries, provides an individual with possibilities limited only by the imagination. Through transportation and refrigeration the exotic has become familiar. There is an infinite variety of floral material at one's fingertips in either its growing or dried form. Any combination of cool relaxing moods or gay enticing flashes can be created by the selection of materials. In designing, a person can be as subtle or as flamboyant as he chooses. It is to this end that *Free Form — Interpretive Design* is presented.

Free Form — Interpretive Design has its roots in the dawn of history when man began to realize that organization and design could serve his needs most efficiently. Perhaps one of the first steps was to arrange objects used to better advantage. The basic design elements have evolved from this inherent ability to organize and arrange. *Free Form — Interpretive Design* is the application of these design principles (elements) for free expression. For example, when one views any group of objects, furniture, flowers, dried materials, etc., one automatically begins to organize them in a pleasing manner and to arrange them to suit his taste. This expression of taste reflects personality and should be allowed to do so. The arranging is the artistic

30

expression of the mental picture, and to express freely gives distinction. This distinction is achieved through application of fundamental principles in good taste, simplicity, and through use of suitable materials.

Free Form — Interpretive Design fits into any architectural scheme, past or present. Where architectural interior design is functional and where natural elements are considered in designing homes, the structures are open and free. Furniture and accessories are simple and functional. Decorative objects that fill rooms largely for effect are gone. Ornamentations such as carved flowers added to furniture or "gingerbread" added to structures have been replaced by simple elements of form and texture. The containers are also simple, bold, and strong of form, with texture and color to add interest and meaning. All nonessentials are stripped and decorations become subordinate to design. Form logically follows function.

Floral arrangements must meet the new demands of *Free Form — Interpretive Design*. They must be a vital part of the decor and suitable for viewing from any angle, presenting a three dimensional, sculptural effect. The space in which the design carves its pattern is vital to the over-all appearance. In all circumstances the atmosphere created by the architect and the interior designer must be complemented by the arrangement. Fewer arrangements are used, thereby giving more importance to each. A *Free Form — Interpretive Design* then becomes a dramatic, forceful piece demanding attention by its importance, Plate 1, *Grecian Horse*, and Plate 2, *Symphonic Browns*.

To meet this challenge the artist must keep abreast of architectural and decorative trends, and couple with this knowledge a clear understanding of the basic design principles and appreciation of materials.

Since this art is no longer hampered by a set of rules, arrangements can be approached with an open mind. The materials themselves can suggest placement or location can suggest materials.

To provide a basis for understanding *Free Form — Interpretive Design*, it may be well to consider art forms of the past, particularly floral art, and trace a brief history to establish our position today.

Chapter II. History of Floral Art

Chapter II

History of Floral Art

ORIENTAL		B.C.	A.D.	
Chinese	Buddha	500	Today	
Japanese			586	- Today
OCCIDENTAL				
Egyptian		2800- 28		
Grecian		600-146		
Roman		28	325	
Byzantine			325	- 600
Gothic			395	- 1425
Persian			1300	- 1700
Renaissance			1400	- 1600
Flemish - Holland			1550	- 1700
Baroque - Italy			1600	- 1700
Rococo - France			1715	- 1774
Georgian - England			1714	- 1760
Classical Revival			1762	- 1830
Directoire - France			1795	- 1799
Empire - France			1804	- 1815
Regency - England			1811	- 1830
Federal - America			1789	- 1830
Romantic - Victorian			1830	- 1890
American - Garden Club			1910	- Today
Free Form Interpretive Design (Benz) *			1957	- ——

* Introduced by the author:
The Garden Club of Illinois, February 7, 1957
Cleveland Flower Arrangers Club, September 11, 1958
National Council of State Garden Clubs, May 9, 1959
(Dedication of permanent home at National Convention—St. Louis)
Garden Clubs of Atlanta, October 14, 1959
Marianne Scruggs Garden Club, Dallas Women's Club, January 11, 1960

PLATE 5

Oriental Mysticism.

Oriental mysticism illustrates the symbolism in Oriental design. Man's complacency with established forms of worship is seen in the repose of the figurine. Components of life are seen in the beauty of the lotus flower. The accomplishment of man's endeavor is represented by the oval form on the curved, white twig, representing man's road of life. Duality of his nature is in the coiled plastic wire. Mysteries of nature are symbolized in the sunflower seed and Phoenix Bird. All materials rise out of his environment (container).

PLATE 5

35

ORIENTAL DEVELOPMENT

China has rightly been called "The Mother of Gardens." Love of natural beauty and her magnificent scenery gave the Chinese their deep appreciation for flowers and art.

Chinese floral art is suggestive rather than representative. It follows the dictates of nature. The Chinese did not develop schools or masters. Due to the genial, gracious temperament of the Chinese, arrangements were bountiful, lush with material and placed with careless abandon. This can be seen in their prints, screens, and paintings. Several arrangements were often used in combination, expressing love for the art.

In the East, Chinese culture first made use of plant materials to augment and stimulate daily living and religious ceremonies. Buddhist monastaries became the centers of this culture, for the monks were free of having to earn a living. They had time to develop the use of flowers into an art form. The elements and mysteries of nature that surrounded them were expressed in floral symbols. Native materials at hand were used to represent concepts that were beyond understanding. The Buddhist fostered symbolism. This fact is revealed in an old legend which is the answer to many queries as to the origin and use of flowers. The story goes that Buddha was preaching on Mount Ko-zan. There appeared the heavenly King Daibon who offered Buddha a golden lotus blossom and asked him to preach the law. Buddha took the flower, held it in his hand but remained silent. His meditation was not understood by anyone in the assembly but by Kasho, one of his devoted followers, who smiled. The Blessed One said to him, "I have received the wonderful thought of Nirvana, the right law which I shall now give to you. This is called the doctrine of transmuted thought." Flowers then became an important symbol of faith.

Oriental Mysticism, Plate 5, illustrates the symbolism characteristic of Chinese designs. The Phoenix Bird came from Egyptian mythology and permeated the Orient. It is the symbol of immor-

36

tality. In ancient mythology the Phoenix Bird was consumed by fire (death), but arose again (resurrection) and is portrayed in this abstract arrangement. The temple prayer table holds an incense burner with handles of stylized cobra heads, from which the floral story is developed. The dried, bleached sunflower seed-pod is representative of one of the natural elements (the sun) that man has observed. The planting of the seed is associated with life and death — symbol of faith in immortality. Flames and smoke rising upward, represented by the bleached palm leaves, as seen on the stem of the sun flower, envelops man. The flames consumed the Phoenix Bird (represented by the wing pointing downward from the flames into the incense burner) but it rose again and is seen in full flight free of earthly ties.

The entity of man's environment is symbolized in the container. His concepts of life are gathered from his environment. The materials rise above it. His road of life is portrayed by the curved, peeled wisteria branch holding the oval form expressing man's success in using natural materials to serve his basic needs, for example; thatched huts, baskets, etc. This handmade oval form represents order (organization), functional form — design.

Thousands of tiny millet seeds, tinted saffron, are the color of the robes worn by the Buddhist monks who taught man "good." The modern yellow and black plastic wires illustrate the duality of man's nature. The yellow represents good and the black evil. These rise from the same location as the wisteria.

Man's complacency with established form of worship is seen in the repose of the symbolic figure, Buddha, at the left. Beauty of life and nature is symbolized in the golden lotus blossom — purity and eternity.

Japan

Japan (586 - present time). The Japanese are the only group of people dedicated to floral art. Their's is a "way of life," a means by which they practice self-control and humility. This art tells a continuous history which dates from the 6th century. With the introduction of Buddhism, and because of the philosophy of the Japanese people toward harmony with nature, they accepted Chinese teachings without question. Due to their love of nature, a persistence to carry on the ideas of their ancestors, and reverence for their masters they have maintained floral art in its original form. A few modifications did appear but the basic principles remained.

The Japanese symbolize features of their beautiful island scenery, of mountains, rivers, rocks, etc., in floral art. Their basic designs emphasize simplicity and asymmetrical balance with dynamic linear form. They follow the dictates of the growing plant. Blossoms and color are secondary; the arrangements feature the natural growth of plants, thereby presenting the importance of their identity. Classical Japanese design requires that stems originate at one point and remain as one unit for four inches (nemoto) to exemplify growth. This nemoto expresses strength in the arrangement comparable to the trunk of a tree. The function of floral art suggests, but does not display flowers. Often a leaf is torn to simulate insect or storm damage, (Plate 6). In their flower arrangements, the principal part of the design inclines toward the place of honor and the guest; it is prominent and shows detail. The secondary portion indicates the host and is smaller. It supports the main subject and maintains proper balance in spacing. The third portion is an attribute adding interest and tri-dimension.

The Japanese religions (Shintoism and Buddhism) do not recognize a heaven as we know it in Christianity; thus, the terminology of the three main lines of Japanese design — heaven, man and earth — is not correct; however, common usage has established their permanence. The three terms began with Josiah Condor, an English missionary, reading a paper before the London Asiatic Society, and repeating them in his book, "Flowers and the Flower Art of Japan." Later an American missionary, Mary Averill, again repeated these names in her book, "Flower Art of Japan," written in 1910, thus establishing the heaven, man, earth concept in our literature. She also indicated a proportion of $1\frac{1}{2}$ times the container, which was a great aid to Americans in understanding approximate measurements of Oriental design.

The Japanese use visual proportions and balance, eliminating measuring. The character of the growing plant suggests height and proportion. They do not have rules as we know them, except in the modern schools.

Ikebana is a familiar word in Japan and freely interpreted means flower arranging. Its literal translation, "living flowers," probably originates from the Buddhist yearning to prolong or preserve all life. The word *hana*, the English equivalent of which is "flower," includes stems, branches, reeds, grasses, foliage, blossoms, in addition to natural elements, e.g., snow, rocks, water, etc. The love of line in all Oriental art rather than mass or color is perhaps the most salient feature, and is more apparent in their flower arrangements, differentiating their floral art from other countries. They prefer a linear, commonplace gnarled branch, carefully placed to exhibit its graceful flowing line, rather than a group of lovely, massed, brightly colored blossoms. When a flower is used, it presents the growing aspects of the plant. To better understand the Orientals and their high esteem for floral art, study their attitude and philosophy. The Japanese blends himself with nature — his is a philosophy of interpreting nature. The American tends to conquer nature and make it subservient to his desire.

Japan was a closed country, living an isolated, artful existence, until the 20th century when Occidental invasion industrialized the nation. This changed the Japanese business attitudes, but not attitudes toward floral art.

The story is told of a simple farmer in Japan who specialized in chrysanthemums. His were famous throughout the land for their perfection. The Emperor heard of the farmer's fine blossoms and expressed the desire to see them. The farmer and his small family worked many long hours in the fields preparing for the visit. When the Emperor arrived there stood only one perfect blossom. The field of blooming plants had been destroyed. The Emperor knelt before this lone blossom for many hours to enjoy its beauty. We in America would pride ourselves on the number of blossoms and the expanse of the field.

Symbolism in floral art illustrates spiritual attributes as it does in paintings. The Orientals do not paint portraits of people as individuals as we portray them in the West. Their characters are legendary. The Japanese visualize the ideal in portraying their characters and places. An Emperor is painted in a dignified manner, a general brave, a lady refined and a farmer rustic.

The spiritual aspects permeated daily living and symbolism grew to be a significant part of floral art. Their arrangements are an idealization of nature, bringing into harmony the life and growth of plant and man. Not only are the arrangements to depict the growth of plants, but the season, surroundings, and conditions under which they grow.

For example:

THE MATERIALS	*Bamboo*	*— stern quality that bends but does not yield*
	Plum (apricot)	*— courage that blossoms in the Winter while snow is on the ground*
	Japanese orchid (aspidistra)	*— purity which unfolds in solitude*
	Chrysanthemum	*— nobility which possesses wisdom*
THE STAGE	*The future*	*— buds, suggesting future growth*
	The present	*— half-opened flowers or perfect foliage*
	The past	*— mature flowers, pods, or dried leaves*

40

TYPE ARRANGEMENT	*Spring*	*— vital growth of vigorous curves*
	Summer	*— full and spreading, open arrangement*
	Autumn	*— sparse and thin arrangement*
	Winter	*— dormant and bare*

Closely allied to the symbolism of *Ikebana* is the association of certain flowers with tradition, literature, and custom. Every holiday has a special flower or foliage:

New Years	*— pine, white chrysanthemum, nandina*
Doll Festival	*— cherry and peach blossoms*
Boys' Festival	*— iris blossoms*

Nanten — the Japanese word for nandina (N. domestica) has significant meaning at New Years. "Nan" is the term for difficulty and misfortune; "ten" means turning from. In floral art nandina signifies the turning from misfortunes of the old year to the happy future of the new year.

To present an insight to the importance and symbolic meaning in Japanese floral design, this illustration will clarify to the Occidental their interpretation. An American writer once visited a provincial Japanese home to familiarize himself with the interior, their mode of living, and to gain an insight to the general "atmosphere." While sipping tea with his hostess, he became aware of the severity of the interior, noting the only decoration in the room was in the alcove, that being the tokonoma. This decoration consisted of three branches of shrub hanging from a small fish basket which was suspended from a post in the alcove. As a backdrop for the flower arrangement, a long, narrow scroll with lines suggestive of flowing water was used. The branches were bare of leaves and flowers; only a few buds showing touches of color were apparent. He, being acquainted with Japanese etiquette, complimented his hostess on her arrangement. Later, the memory of its sparseness returned many times to the writer's mind. After becoming familiar with Japanese

41

flower arrangements and symbolism, he realized that, though the whole composition was bare and the family he had visited was living in moderate circumstances, the subtlety contrived in this arrangement foretold the family's salute to oncoming Spring. The kakemono (scroll) suggested the melting snows and flowing streams. The bud-bearing branches of plum tree were suggestive of early Spring bursting into bloom while snow was still on the ground.

The *Ikenobo* or classical school preserves the tradition of the original concept of *Ikebana* which began in the 6th century. The *Ikenobo* school developed the three segments, *Shin* (spiritual truth), *Soe* (harmonizer), and *Tai* (material substance). These segments are known to the Occidental as heaven, man, and earth. The groups form an asymmetrical triangle. The first is an upright group, heaven ($1\frac{1}{2}$ to 3 times the container); the second an intermediate group, man (approximately $\frac{2}{3}$ length of heaven), leaning away from the upright; and the third is lower, earth (about $\frac{1}{2}$-$\frac{1}{3}$ of man), on the opposite side and also leaning forward. The various modern schools have their own specific measurements for each division.

In Plate 6, Classical Ikenobo Aspidistra, Japanese orchid foliage is arranged in the classical style of the *Ikenobo* school. The container, an antique ogencho, is placed on a kwadai, which is proper for the display of the arrangement. This photograph shows the side view in order that the placement of the stems forming the nemoto can be clearly seen. The front view would appear to have one stem. The tallest line (Shin) originates in the center of the container, gracefully curves upward, ending directly over the point of origin. The addition of a leaf to either side are attributes, adding interest, strength, and rhythmically descending to the man line (Soe). A leaf is torn to indicate ravages of nature. The eye then follows smoothly into the third group (Tai) in which there are graceful accentuated curves, symbolic of earth rhythms.

Fig. 1

The front view of a Classical Ikenobo arrangement showing the nemoto as one stem.

42

PLATE 6

Classical Ikenobo — Aspidistra

The original concept of Ikebana is exemplified in this design. The three segments (heaven, man and earth) shin — spiritual truth, soe — harmonizer, and tai — material substance, form the asymmetrical triangle characteristic of classical Japanese design.

During the 15th century the ruling military leaders practiced the arts. They felt the need of a religion that would be simple for camp life. They found this in the *Zen* sect of Buddhism. The attainment of *Zen* is aimed at the harmony of man and nature. It was during this period that the tea ceremony, *Cha-No-Yu,* was perfected. Simplicity and naturalism marked a deviation from the staid formal life and affected the arts. The tokonoma or alcove was also developed during this period in the main room of the home. It became popular for even the most humble dwelling to have a recessed wall portion or tokonoma — the place of honor for a cherished possession, a kakemono (scroll), or a flower arrangement. No more than three decorative objects are placed in this alcove at one time, each carefully selected and placed to achieve maximum harmony. This created a new change in flower arranging. Cha-bana or tea-flower and *Nageire* "thrown-in" designs emerged (Plate No. 7). This form was more in keeping with the simple life and humble dwellings. The tokonoma became a place of study and meditation. The kakemono was hung in this alcove complementing the flower arrangement. It was generally a poem or painting depicting the season and constituted a favorite gift to the bride.

In Plate 7, *Summer San-ju-giri,* a san-ju-giri (three level bamboo container) is selected for the *Nageire* arrangement to express informality, simplicity, and naturalism showing change from the formal *Ikenobo* school. The plant material is representative of the three regions: Camellia foliage expresses upright growth on the hillsides; the gracefully flowing, descending branches of the pomegranate suggest plants overhanging the rock cliffs; the center flower, day-lily, is from the meadow land, and callas placed in the lower section are indicative of the lake region. The three segments, Shin, Soe, Tai, are maintained. Note the flow of line originating in the callas, directing the eye upward into the camellia foliage, then down into the natural placement of the pomegranate branches which complete the circulation. The base, shiki-ita, is made of woven bamboo. The Oriental visualizes the three regions represented in the container and the plant materials which may recall many happy experiences of Summer.

With the introduction of the Western flora, which generally had short stems, a new form of *Ikebana* developed. This was the third great deviation from the formal style of the *Ikenobo* school. Unshin Ohara recognized its value and developed a freer design form called *Moribana* style (piled-up flowers). He maintained the three segments, but placed them in a low-type container, a suipan or sunabachi, which permitted greater abundance of flowers and foliage

44

than the more severe predecessors. He divided the three main groupings in their placement in the container. Naturalness of growth prevailed. This school was handed down to his son, Koun Ohara, in 1916 and to the grandson, Houn, in 1938.

In Plate 8, *Mountain Stream*, the sunabachi conjures much mysticism and symbolism for the development of this floral picture. Large rocks represent the mountains from which rise the plant materials. The agapanthus blossoms (Shin and Soe), give strength by their firm placement and restricted curves. The attributes, papyrus and hosta foliage, are placed to form a strong nemoto. The papyrus repeat the radiating formation of the agapanthuses. The solid plane of the hosta leaf adds weight to this main line, repeats the formation

45

PLATE 8
Mountain Stream

A Moribana arrangement is developed in the sunabachi. Large rocks represent the mountains from which rise plant materials. Agapanthus blossoms (shin and soe) are reinforced with papyrus and hosta foliage. Papyrus repeat the radiating umbel of the agapanthus. Low growing liriope (tai) is grouped separately. The space between the two groups is suggestive of the mountain stream, called, in Japan, "a place for the fish to swim through."

of the rocks, and its veining complements the radiating line of its companions. The "Tai" grouping has been arranged separately, allowing space between the main grouping which is suggestive of the mountain stream, and as the Japanese say, "a place for the fish to swim through." This low growing liriope (L. muscari), with its foliage was selected to represent "Tai"; it repeats the color of the main blossoms.

It was my great fortune to be a guest in the home of Houn Ohara-san, one of the great floral masters of Japan, whose grandfather initiated this third great change in *Ikebana*. Upon arriving I was ushered into the main room of his lovely home. It was bare except for a table and pillows in the center of the room. In the toko-

46

noma was a flower arrangement in my honor. Custom required me to sit before the alcove quietly before speaking and admire the work done to welcome me. While I was doing so, the Master entered. No word was spoken until I had time to meditate on the flower arrangement. After due time I turned and my host greeted me. Then it was appropriate for me to express my joy and appreciation. This ceremony is strictly observed with all visiting friends and those visiting in their country — seldom is an Occidental so honored in a Japanese home. They are usually taken out to be entertained and not invited into the private home.

Many schools sprang up to teach the Westerner the art of Japanese floral design. Each Japanese Master has his own conception of arranging and his own set of rules and measurements. Within each school there is much variation from the classical art form. Today, as in America, there is a tremendous urge for freedom, a strong force for the modern or abstract. The floral masters of Japan are going toward *Free Form — Interpretive Design* and even bizarre designs. They are somewhat puzzling to the Occidental, for we do not see the reason and logic in their interpretation. Although many contemporary pieces of art are still puzzling to the untrained eye, they are considered masterpieces. An art form will develop from this rebellion just as new art forms in painting and sculpture emerged some years ago in France. We owe a great debt to Oriental design for our employment of line and proportion.

PLATE 9

Chinese Family Altar

This antique container is a Chinese family altar. In the bowl, incense is burned during the ritual. Scotch broom maintains the three segments of Oriental design but pink floribunda roses in a naturalistic design are added to suit American taste.

47

OCCIDENTAL DEVELOPMENT

During the Egyptian period (2800-28 B. C.) tombs were profusely decorated with pictures of flowers showing bouquets that were carried or held aloft in bowls. Early Egyptians loved fragrance and grew sweet scented flowers. Water cooled this arid country in which water lilies, lotus, and papyrus were plentiful. Their paintings showed flowers and fruit in flat orderly repetitive patterns, for they had no knowledge of perspective or depth in illustration. Flowers and foliage were alternated to produce a feeling of quantity. One flower was often inserted in another (abstract form) to express and reflect the lush growth of the Nile.

In Plate 10, *Egypt,* the Egyptian pyramids are seen in the shape of the container; it establishes the pattern for the pyramidal form of the floral arrangement. The foliage repeats the points of the pyramid. The silhouette pattern of the strelitzia flowers implies the hieroglyphics of their painting and recalls the history of the era. Their placement is taken from paintings found on the walls of tombs and from carvings of stone at Luxor. The orange color of the petals reflects the brilliant sun and arid countryside, with a touch of blue in the blossom reflecting the color of the sky. The echeveria is representative of the plant growth in this country of little rainfall, and repeats the colors of the purple-gray container symbolizing the end of this period in history. The stylized figurine, whose exaggerated sculptured form is contemporary, is also representative of the drawings. The position of elbows combines with the peak of the high hair style repeating the three points. The use of three (echeveria) and seven (4 birds-of-paradise and 3 leaves) in number is suggestive of early ritualism and religion. Formal balance and repetition are characteristic of the period.

PLATE 10
Egypt

Egyptian pyramids are seen in the shape of the container and floral pattern. Foliage repeats the pyramidal form. Strelitzia flowers etch hieroglyphics as seen in the tombs of the Pharaohs propitiating spirits symbolized by the stylized figure. The use of three (echeveria) and seven (4 birds-of-paradise and 3 leaves) in number is suggestive of early ritualism and religion.

Grecian

Perhaps the greatest advancement in art came during the Grecian period (600-146 B.C.). The Greeks developed the finest sculptural and architectural advances the world has ever known. Their culture, art, and political science have never been surpassed. They worshipped and idealized the human form, exemplifying it in all decorations and sculpture. Their stone carvings were so delicately executed that drapery covering a body appeared so sheer one could almost feel the texture of the material and the skin it covered. *Nike* (5th century B. C.), the Goddess of Victory, removing one of her sandals, and *Venus de Milo* are two of the finest examples of Grecian art (Plate No. 11).

Their athletes were adorned with wreaths and garlands similar to those used today in the Olympic Games. Flowers were offered in these forms and in baskets. Description of flowers appears in Grecian literature, especially in its poetry. Flowers with particular meaning were dedicated to Greek gods. The acanthus leaf was used as a motif to decorate and adorn the capital of the Corinthian column.

The shadow box arrangement, Plate 11, *Grecian Splendor*, portrays the story of the magnificence of ancient Greece. The Acropolis is represented by the barren branches carrying the eye to the figure, Venus de Milo, which is silhouetted and free of materials. Fruit and flowers are placed in a naturalistic design depicting the lush growth of the period. The classic Grecian column is perfect for the container.

Sculpture in the 5th century B. C. discarded the archaic static form for realistic, marble representations which we know as Classical. Sculpture of the Grecian period had strength and was bold in form. Motion became a vital element in their art. Plate 1, *Grecian Horse*, embodies the glories of the period in its stately carriage. It is clean cut, bold, and definite. Only the races in which it ran and the rider are left to the imagination. The flower arrangement in abstract is the perfect tribute to this great piece of art. The

PLATE 11

Grecian Splendor

Venus de Milo portrays the magnificence of Grecian culture. The Acropolis is represented by bleached branches carrying the eye to the figure. Fruit and flowers are placed in a naturalistic design depicting the lush growth of this spectacular period.

original of this stately chariot horse, fashioned of bronze, is a splendid example of Grecian art, circa 470 B. C., and is now in the Metropolitan Museum of Art. This cast is probably the most important single object in the classical collection of this Museum. The modeling has just that combination of realism and stylization with which Grecian art of the second half of the fifth century achieved its greatest triumphs. It was made when Greece, after subduing the Persians, entered its greatest century of culture. Whether this horse once formed part of a chariot group or had a rider is now impossible to say. The rendering of the mouth suggests that it was being pulled by reins and the mark part way down the neck indicates that there was once a bridle. This statuette is tangible evidence of an immortal and ageless beauty that is unchanged by the passage of centuries. The study of this horse made the search for floral material ever more demanding and zestful. It was a challenge. The development is one of the thrills of this art — here pure design is expressed

51

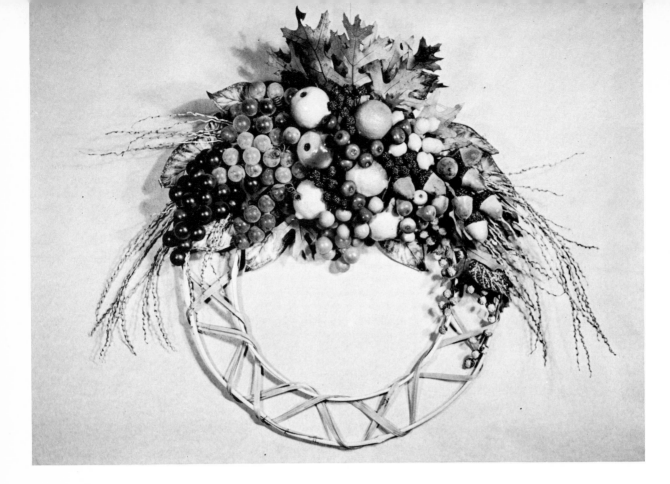

PLATE 12
Roman Wreath

The reed wreath is representative of materials available to the Romans. It is interlaced with thongs by which they strapped on their sandals and is also suggestive of ribbons tying on foliage in della Robia fashion. Vigor and rich abundance is shown in fruit and foliage.

through sculptured material. The motion of this steed made it even more demanding. Allium blossoms, dried and painted gold (depicting the golden age of the period) fulfill all requirements. The carriage of the head is immediately recognizable in the forward blossom. The lines of allium reproduce the body lines of the horse with the main piece slanting into the container, giving force of motion created by the legs of the statuette. The vertical allium suggests the rider poised slightly forward for motion, giving balance to counteract the force of movement. The lilies have perfect structural form to repeat the smooth, clean-cut curves of the arched neck and hips. These are used in abstract form and placed at an angle to emphasize forward motion — what flower, other than trumpet-shaped, could serve this purpose? The abstract form of lilies represents the Olympic torch which is used today. The container with its texture, color, and form blends with the featured art piece and picks up the interesting pitted effect of the allium flowers. It is a stylized chalice such as used in the Grecian era. Each unit has its own base emphasizing

52

its importance. The horse has greater eye appeal, so a second block was added under the container. There is perfect harmony of all units — a story is told yet no one unit dominates. The focus is on the story and complete composition. Purism in design is the reward of such blending. Rarely does one find materials that complement each other to such a high degree.

Roman

The Romans were conquerors and contributed little to the arts, but borrowed heavily from the Greeks. During the Roman period (28 B. C.-325 A. D.) the garland as a decorative motif was perfected. A beautiful example can be found in the garland carved in the Ara Pacis (Altar of Peace, 14 B. C.) to honor the emperor Augustus. A similar floral motif is used today in America at Thanksgiving and Christmas. The artists of the Italian Renaissance were inspired by these carvings as expressed by the Italian artists Andres and Luca della Robia whose wreaths are familiar.

In Plate 12, *Roman Wreath*, the stylized reed wreath form is used and is representative of the materials which were available to the Romans. The framework is interlaced with thongs in the manner in which they strapped on their sandals and is also suggestive of the ribbons tying on foliage in della Robia fashion. The abundance of grasses, fruits, and autumn foliage are representative of the period.

In Plate 13, *Roman Garland*, the garland that appeared on Ara Pacis has been used as a decorative motif since the Renaissance. In this Plate, the garland motif has been stylized on a diamond shaped plaque in keeping with the contemporary demands of today. The curled and pointed aspidistra foliage suggest the linear background of the original garland. Grasses, okra seed pods, cecropia (C. peltate), leaves form a group, and for the center of interest artichoke is used with an accent of Christmas ornaments in gold, suggestive of grapes. Garlands and wreaths are used extensively in Christmas decorations.

PLATE 13
Roman Garland

This stylized garland meets the contemporary demands of today. Garlands were used profusely by the Romans as decorative motifs and at ceremonials.

53

Byzantine

The Byzantine period (325-600 A. D.) exhibited strong tendencies toward formality. This arid country was influenced by both Occidental and Oriental cultures. They contributed the cone and spiral design in foliage, using fruit and flowers in clusters or garlands around the cone.

In Plate No. 14, *Baccarat Byzantine Cone,* using the floral contributions of the Byzantine period (the formal cone) for inspiration, this contemporary design illustrates the transition of periods. Rarely does one see harmony result in the transitional design where elements of established good taste and usage of former periods (Byzantine and Persian) are employed to provide an effect of boldness and freshness to a later period (Georgian-Neoclassic). The spiral of the Baccarat crystal candelabrum lends a feeling of the Turkish minaret holding aloft the contemporary floral design — a cone of snapdragons belted with callas culminating with the motion in the vertical taper. Swirling motion in space is created.

Gothic

During the Gothic period (395-1425 A. D.) feudalism, wars, unrest and general disquiet left little leisure time for flowers per se. Small herb gardens were grown within monastary walls for culinary use. The only floral motifs appeared as art forms on the ornate religious manuscripts of the church. The Gothic arch in architecture was the greatest single contribution of this era.

Persian

The Persians' (1300-1700 A. D.) love for gardens and flowers is still seen in the beautiful Mogul gardens in Kashmir. The Mountain Station, as it is called, has several exquisite gardens representative of this period. The Moguls collected trees and plants from their wanderings and incorporated them into their estates. These Persian rulers so loved their gardens that they had their craftsmen weave their favorite garden scenes into elaborate colored carpets. These were not used as rugs but as wall hangings in order that they might

54

enjoy the beauty of Spring through the winter months.

Neshat — meaning Garden of Pleasure, Cheshmi Sha-hi — Royal Springs, and Shalimar — Garden of Moon Love, is the most magnificent of all. Shalimar was built by the Emperor Jehangir for his favorite wife, Nur-Jeman. The design is said to be a copy of the famous carpet, "Choroes Spring," in possession of Choroes 1, the Sassanian Emperor of Iran 531-579 A. D. The background representing the soil was woven in gold thread, the water sewn in crystals, and the flowers and trees were set in precious stones.

The papier-maché work perfected in this period remains on the ceiling of the pavillion, clearly showing the garden flowers. It is in Shalimar that one of the unique features in landscape design is perfected. The water cascades over candlelit falls into quiet reflecting basins and then over arabesque slabs — that of stone, carved into intricate designs — which control cascading water. The water, in its turbulence, weaves herringbone patterns with borders of scallops. The overall picture is that of a carpet woven with water. Nowhere else in the world is such art exemplified or employed. Flower beds, in profuse bloom, border the water gardens and add color. The Persians, however, did not know floral composition and arrangement in a definite plan.

Renaissance

The Renaissance (1400-1600 A. D.) was a period of transition and of hunger for knowledge and beauty. It was a period of intellectual re-birth, changes in attitude, and moral living. Western nations emerged with vitality from the Dark Ages. Until this time the patron of the arts was either the church or nobility. Flowers were used as incidental fill-in or as a decorative motif. No importance was given the blossom as subject matter until the 16th-17th centuries.

However, economic conditions changed. The discovery of the new world encouraged commerce and with it the introduction of new plants which gave pride in horticulture. The bourgeois man became

important in business. New social trends emerged, the middle class gained in position and became interested in culture. No longer did religion dominate the arts. Until this period in history the arts and guidance of culture were held by a comparatively few ruling families and the church. There was a new interest in and a rediscovery of the classical art forms of Greece and Rome. The Renaissance influence reached its peak in Italy, spread to France, England, and then to the rest of the continent. Florence was the center of this movement. Its ruling families patronized the arts, giving impetus to its advancement. Cosimo and Lorenzo de Medici founded the Biblioteca Medicea Laurenziana and the Platonic Academy. Here artists were trained who spread their knowledge throughout the continent. The church and noble families patronized such masters as Donatello, Ghiberti, and Luca della Robbia.

Baroque — ITALY

From 1600 to 1700 A. D., culture and classicism of the Roman influence gave way to the creative imagination of the artist. Broken curves, dynamic contrasts and elaborately ornamented decorations were introduced in architecture. From Italy came the della Robbia wreath and the book, *Flora*, by Giovanni Battisti Gerrari, Rome, 1633, which told of arranging flowers in flowing formal style.

During the Renaissance period cherubs were used in profusion to add an ethereal motif to their art. In Plate 15, *Florentine Elegance*, following the dictates of the Renaissance period, a crystal bowl is used as a container, held aloft by a cherub. The phalaenopsis orchids form the flowing formal lines of the floral pattern as described in the book mentioned above. Roses are massed in a graceful "S" curve with bells-of-Ireland accentuating this line. This floral material expresses the extravagance of the period in which art reached its zenith. Cherub candelabra are used as accent accessories.

PLATE 15
Florentine Elegance

Flowing formal lines of the floral pattern and the cherub motif exemplifies the Italian Renaissance.

57

Flemish — HOLLAND

Holland, during the period 1550-1700, A.D., was a wealthy nation of merchants and seafaring men who developed an appetite for pictures of themselves and their way of life. The artists were specialists either in portraits or landscapes; then later in this period the everyday subjects and still-lifes came into vogue. Floral paintings were highly prized for their beauty. Flowers were the main subject and not incidental as background fill-ins. Floral painting shows the richness of this period and clearly depicts the great variety of blossoms that were prized. Strong color and form expressed Baroque energy and vitality. It was during this era that books disseminated horticultural information which gave impetus to the horticultural pride. The tulip became so popular that prices soared to great heights — fortunes were won and lost on the sale of rare varieties. Flemish style is characterized by the massing of flowers in a graceful manner, combining rich colors in warm tones, using birds' nests with eggs, fruit, shells, and a number of everyday objects. The predominant colors are tones of red, deep yellow, violet, blue, and orange. This was an important period concerning flowers for they gained as subject matter and were appreciated for their intrinsic value.

Plate No. 16, *Fifteenth Century-Dutch,* is an example of the European bouquet type arrangement. A classical urn is used; however, during this period they did not follow "pattern" in their floral arrangements. In this design, pattern is developed. Line flowers, pink snapdragons, give the proportion and form the oval design including the base of the container. Mass flowers form a complete circle with the round portion of the container. There is a triangle of red roses bisected with an "S" curve of tulips, terminating with a cluster of grapes. Dark purple anemones are placed at the center of interest. The patterns in this mass design are harmoniously interwoven. Note that the left handle is free in order for the complete shape of the urn to be suggested. The bird accessory gives an authentic note to the design due to the associational value it implies. Dutch paintings of flowers often incorporated birds with their nests in the compositions. The tip of the snapdragon directs the eye into the tail of the bird and this line is carried back into the flowers by the curve of its body and head. Although the flowers are massed, each retains its individuality indicative of the early nursery prints in the catalogues of this era.

Rococo — FRANCE

Rococo decor (1715-1744 A. D.), originating in France, superceded the heavy grandeur of the Baroque (Italy 1600-1700 A. D.), but carried over its design characteristic of curves. It was welcomed, for it added gaiety, youth, and vigor. There was a delicacy, absolute freedom, rhythmic irregularity, and somewhat feminine touch with flowing lines and reverse curves. Flower arrangements were used in great abundance in daily living and festive occasions. The colors were delicate to match the dainty work of the period. The forms found in shells, scrolls and flowers defined the art decoration of interiors and furniture. This period received its name from the French word "rocaille" meaning shell which was a main decorative motif. This period reached its height with the reign of Louis XV in the early 18th century. It was during this time that Chinese art added bizarre motifs to the style and spread to other countries. The word "Chinoiserie" was used to describe the Oriental influence. The furniture maker Chippendale was greatly impressed and this influence is still seen today in furniture.

In Plate 60, *Chinoiserie*, the Chinese pagoda and Goddess definitely state the Far Eastern influence. They set in motion the rhythmic curves which establish the main floral pattern — the Hogarth curve. The flowing "S" curve, or "Line of Beauty," is developed with dried sea plume reinforced with okra pods and artichoke blossoms. Teasel burrs and lotus pods give textural interest. All materials are dried, painted white, and covered with mother-of-pearl.

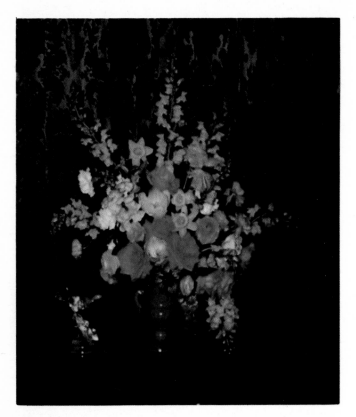

PLATE 16

Fifteenth Century — Dutch

This is an example of European bouquet type arrangement. "Pattern" is developed within a pattern. Line flowers give proportion and form the oval design with mass flowers making a complete circle. A triangle of red roses bisect the "S" curve of tulips terminating with a cluster of grapes creating interesting geometric patterns within the oval. The bird accessory adds authenticity to the Dutch floral painting.

PLATE 18

The Three Graces

This composition derives its name from the Grecian statues showing influence of Classic revival in the Rococo period. The container is fluted seashells which gave the period its name. Irregular curves, flowing lines, and dainty filigree work are characteristic of the period.

PLATE 17

A Sèvres Porcelain

Larkspurs form a symmetrical triangle expressing strength which artisans began to show in their work. Pink roses and blue irises severely cut the design. The bronze framework of the container replaces the flowing lines of the former period. Stronger color also expresses this strength.

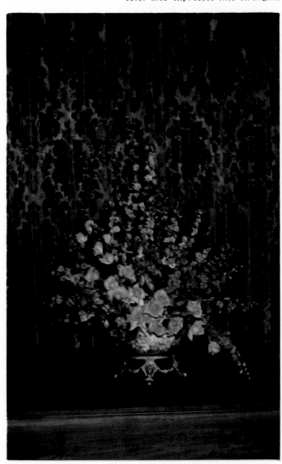

60

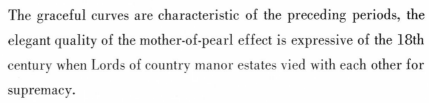

The graceful curves are characteristic of the preceding periods, the elegant quality of the mother-of-pearl effect is expressive of the 18th century when Lords of country manor estates vied with each other for supremacy.

During the latter part of the Rococo period there was another revival of Classical art. The irregular curves, flowing lines and dainty filigree work had begun to lose their fascination. Plate 18, *The Three Graces* — This composition derives its name from the Grecian statues which show the influence of Classical revival. These form the pedestal for the container of fluted sea shells. Curving Scotch broom, painted white and covered with mother-of-pearl, continues the flowing, graceful curves characteristic of the era. Cymbidium orchids counterbalance the height of the Scotch broom on the opposite side and carry the eye into the figures. Lily-of-the-valley and bouvardia accent this line and add dainty texture while camellias and roses give needed mass to this design.

In France during the Renaissance, Rococo remained a court style and was essentially luxuriant. The rich fabrics, tapestries, and ornate furniture were copied throughout Europe. Pottery development reached its peak in the porcelains of Sèvres. Fine porcelains and bronze containers were placed in niches or on pedestals. Epergnes were used frequently for banquets and state dinners to give importance to floral bouquets.

Toward the end of the Louis XVI reign a more masculine appearance exerted itself. The Sèvres porcelain was encased in bronze framework which is a deviation from the delicacy and gaiety of the former period. In Plate 17, *A Sèvres Porcelain*, the floral pattern expresses the strength that the artisans wished to show during this era. A solid triangular pattern was used to meet the demand. Pink larkspur establishes the equilateral triangle with darker pink roses forming a diagonal "S" curve across the design, carrying the eye to the figures painted on the porcelain container. Deep blue irises are used to express strength with color, rather than the dainty blues of the preceding period.

Georgian — ENGLAND

The Georgian period (1714-1760) was influenced by foreign lands. People began to travel extensively. It was fashionable to adorn the home with collections from other countries, yet definite composition of floral design had not been established. Flowers were admired for horticultural perfection only.

The artist, William Hogarth (1697-1764), painted a portrait of himself and his dog, Trump. In a lower corner of this painting he had drawn, on a palette, a serpentine curve with the words, "The Line of Beauty." This phrase stimulated many discussions concerning the meaning. To establish and more or less justify his concept of "fluctuating ideas of taste," he documented his ideas in a treatise called "Analogy of Beauty" in 1753. The lazy "S" (Hogarth curve) has had a great influence on design in America. The curved line is appreciated in all art and in the human form. It is often said that in any flower show the Hogarth pattern is universally preferred and will never fail to impress a viewer.

In 1740, nursery prints commissioned by Furber and painted by Peter Casteels were widely circulated. No floral pattern was apparent for they merely illustrated the flowers of the month. This did, however, have some bearing on arrangements. Flowers were used in practically all art forms, especially in portraiture and religious themes.

The English were fond of horticulture. Lavish gardens and stately manor houses were at their height. The architect, George Adams, greatly influenced design. Fine furniture makers such as Chippendale, Sheraton, and Hepplewhite contributed magnificent styles that to this day remain some of the finest in design. Wedgewood perfected his pottery and Sheffield, England, became known for its silver plate. Both added substantially to floral accessories.

PLATE 19
Victorian Fruit

A French compote of gold is embellished with cherubs holding a shell whose ornament is a sea goddess. Sea plumes in natural shades of purple and mauve have been highlighted with metallic glitter. The fruit, also covered with metallic sparkle in brilliant jewel tones, is expressive of the lavishness of the era.

Aspiration PLATE 20

In Plate 20, *Aspiration,* a tall chalice lends itself beautifully to the development of the aspiring linear pattern in the floral design. This pattern is suggestive of the Hogarth curve. The line of yellow snapdragons flows gracefully into repetitious placement of daffodils, and is completed with the sequence of yellow tulips and green grapes. Deeper yellow ranunculi add weight to the composition, tying the converging lines of the other flowers. The silver plateau adds elegance to this stately design.

64

In Plate 21, *The Line of Beauty*, drama is created in developing the Hogarth line of beauty with four types of material, each complete in pattern and superimposed upon the other. Pussy-willow establishes the outline and is reinforced by phalaenopsis orchids; bells-of-Ireland repeat the outline of the "S" curve of pink roses and create an interesting cross-diagonal pattern. Distinction and originality are portrayed by the skillful handling of the floral patterns developed by each kind of material, yet blended so carefully that one flows into the other.

PLATE 22
French Neoclassical

Transition of periods is shown in this design. The flowing lines have been replaced with restricted geometric curves.

PLATE 21 *The Line of Beauty*

Classical

Classic Revival — Neoclassic (1762-1830) influenced the arts and architecture in Europe and the United States during the late 18th and early 19th centuries and prevailed in the United States until it gave way to the Victorian period. Interest in antiquity gained impetus with the discovery of Pompeii. The English architect, archaeologist and painter, James Stuart, who visited Athens in 1751 with Nicholas Revett, wrote a volume, "Classical Antiquities of Athens," which greatly influenced the Classical Revival.

Art became more decisive. Straight lines of Roman and Greek architecture replaced Baroque and Rococo curves. The new curves were geometric and clean-cut. The furniture became sturdy. Flower containers were mounted on metal or marble mounts and placed on pedestals and columns. Roman and Greek forms were at their height. The garland reappeared in a more delicate form. Wedgewood showed the classical influence by using the Grecian figures, garlands and urns in his designing. These motifs were used profusely on all his ware.

Neoclassicism, toward the end of its period, became heavier, the colors darker and much gold trim was used. In France, Directoire preceded Empire style which was in vogue through the Napoleonic era. In England it was known as Regency, and in America this period was known as Federal.

In Plate 22, *French Neoclassic,* using an antique container of French classical influence, the floral arrangement is suggestive of the flowing lines of previous periods, however, a more severe treatment has been given the pattern. The vertical position of the snapdragons which is repeated by the ranunculi blossoms is given a slight curve. Strength is gained by the addition of pink caladium foliage which adds weight and gives color contrasts. The arrangement shows the transition of the Neoclassical periods.

Directoire

The Directoire period (1795-1799), although short, exerted strong influence on cultural decor. This era was a transition between the time of Louis XVI and Napoleon's reign. Aristocratic ornateness of the Louis regime gave way to an enthusiastic emphasis on classic form. Tapestries were replaced with either plain, painted wall surfaces or decorative wallpaper. Furniture began to show strength in its geometric curves and sturdy appearances, omitting the delicate French curves.

Empire

Empire decor (1804-1815) was characterized by the success of the First French Empire under Napoleon. As a result of his victorious campaigns, Roman and Egyptian motifs were used profusely. Roman classic form symbolized grandeur and imperial pomp. All traces of any former feminine influence disappeared; the court of Napoleon was definitely masculine. Chief ornamentations were mounts of bronze, ormolu, and brass. The laurel wreath in gold appeared in tapestries, on pedestals, and containers. Other emblems were the obelisk, winged griffin, lion and the bee. Flowers, grown as horticultural specimens, or for arrangements, were not important in this period, Plate 44 *Formal Tea* .

Regency

Robert Adams, a famous architect whose great influence in design characterizes this period of British history, visited Roman ruins and noted buildings of the Italian Renaissance, returning to England to

67

construct and decorate stately manor houses. He provided niches, alcoves and bays for exquisite statuary and classic urns. The arts, literature, and architecture flourished at this time. This was a period of elegance.

Federal

America was a new republic and patriotism was at its height. Duncan Phyfe, an outstanding furniture maker, through his designs immediately recalls this period in American history known as Federal. He was influenced by the English cabinetmakers, Hepplewhite and Sheraton. The young Republic depended heavily on importations for interior decor, e.g., wall coverings and accessories. France, her friendly ally, was favored. Silver epergnes, tiered arrangements of fruit and flowers, and patriotic emblems were in vogue, especially the American spread eagle.

Romantic

The Romantic, Victorian Period (1830-1890) ushered in a change of living. The average man began to gain fortunes which resulted in extravagant living in all phases of life. Over-indulgence and lavish living marked this period of history. Colors were rich with much trim in gold on the containers, furnishings, etc. Jewel tones predominated. Nothing of note was added to interior design or architecture. In Plate 19, *Victorian Fruit*, the French compote of gold is embellished with cherubs and a shell ornamented with a sea-goddess reigns supreme. Sea plumes in natural shades of purple and mauve have been highlighted with metallic glitter. The fruit also has been covered with metallic sparkle in brilliant jewel tones expressive of the Victorian era.

In Plate 23, *Victorian Shadow Box*, the gold framed shadow box with a background of purple velvet establishes the color preference of the Victorian period. The highly decorative container with touches of gold holds an arrangement of pink begonia blossoms with their foliage. Pale pink phalaenopsis present the floral motif which

68

PLATE 23
Victorian Shadow Box

Highly decorative container with touches of gold holds an arrangement of pink begonia blossoms with pale pink phalaenopsis embracing the lovely jeweled fan and terminating with a tussy-muzzy of violets. The gold framed shadow box with a background of purple velvet is representative the color preference of this period.

embraces the lovely jeweled fan as a part of the arrangement and terminating with the tussy-muzzy of violets.

During the Victorian era, "set" flower groupings were massed. Often the flowers were dried and placed under glass domes. All flowers were given sentimental meanings. Each carried a message of devotion or love. It was fashionable to carry tussy-muzzies or colonial bouquets as we know them. This was a prelude to the present day use of corsages for personal adornment. Fruits were often used with flowers in groupings. In Plate 86, *Georgian Epergne*, the wall covering is silk damask of a rich burgundy color and framed with architectural features of pilasters expressing the elegance of the Victorian period. The epergne holds a design of dark red, velvet-textured roses, lily-of-the-valley, camellias, and violets portraying the lavishness of the period. The side arms hold tuzzy-muzzy arrangements of violets and sweetheart roses expressing the sentimental feeling attributed to flowers.

American

From the study of the preceding Occidental eras, one sees that floral art forms have always leaned toward the bouquet type in flower arranging. They are prone to let the individual develop his own talent. Europeans did not have the leisure time to devote to hobbies or avocations. They are not "club joiners" as we are in America, therefore, their floral arrangements and design did not develop pattern or a set of rules and regulations. The European art form has been characterized by quantity of flowers and massed designs. The trend was toward specimen blossoms rather than planned arrangements. Selected blossoms were grouped to illustrate horticultural advances rather than to create design or to express an idea.

Prior to 1900, flower arranging in America was not the distinct art that it is considered today. Horticultural specimens were still preferred. They were used for various social occasions and widely for medicinal purposes. Flowers did not attain the great symbolism that early Egyptians, Grecians or Orientals attributed to them. In 1914, Liberty Hyde Bailey's "Standard Cyclopedia of Horticulture" mentions some of the principles of design. Later the garden clubs began to include classes for artistic arrangements in flower shows held mainly for horticultural interest. After World War I this art gained much impetus from the Garden Club movement. These clubs made great strides in improving the community's natural beauty. Numerous articles and books on the subject began to appear. Geometric design in floral art became established.

In Plate 24, *Easter Elegance,* an oval geometrical pattern is developed in the antique Victorian crystal lamp base. White larkspurs establish the outline of the pattern and form the background for the development of the diagonal line of Easter lilies and majestic daisies. Caladium foliage is used within the oval pattern to add accent and force to the line of lilies. Majestic daisies are a transitional note in texture between the lilies and the larkspurs.

PLATE 24

Easter Elegance

The antique Victorian lamp base holds an oval geometric pattern developed with white larkspurs. A diagonal line of Easter lilies, reinforced with majestic daisies, bisects the pattern. Caladium foliage is used within the arrangement adding force to the line of Easter lilies.

PLATE 24

In Plate 87, *Formal Balance,* the triangular design is developed. It is preferred for formal occasions. This classic epergne of the Napoleonic period, the griffins showing Egyptian influence from his campaigns, is an excellent container for the strong equilateral triangle. Blue irises establish the points of the triangle. The composition is completed with a selection of daffodils, ranunculi, and tulips.

In Plate 25, *Fuji and Cordyline,* the asymmetrical triangle is developed to exemplify the third geometrical pattern. Since natural balance was the influence of the Orient, the Fuji chrysanthemums, which are named for the sacred mountain of Japan, Fujiyama, are used. Cordyline foliage repeats the asymmetrical pattern and adds interest by its contrast in texture to the Fuji chrysanthemums. A bowl similar to a rice bowl is used as a container. The flamingo figures create a parallel to the hypotenuse of the triangle.

From the Japanese we borrowed the principle of line, asymmetrical balance, appreciation of nature, and measurements of flower stems in relation to container to gain good proportion. From our Western heritage mass grouping of flowers for decorative effects and formal design were added. Americans began serious study of color from a scientific, psychological, and practical point of view. Color was appreciated and became an integral part of design. A geometrical style with set rules was then developed. America became design conscious.

Since the American home shows the influence of many countries we borrow from all to reproduce flower arrangements suggestive of a period in history or of that country. Scarcity of literature on the subject forces an arranger to depend on past art works, poetry, literature, bas-relief, painting, mosaics, etc., that were rich in the floral presentations. Research indicates that through the ages no definite floral patterns were established, except in Japan, until America developed the geometrical form which combined the line

PLATE 25
Fuji and Cordyline

Tri-colored ti leaves form the graceful asymmetrical pattern and background for the soft pink Fuji blossoms. Flamingos add a feeling of naturalness and informality repeating the color note of the blossoms and foliage.

72

PLATE 25

of Japanese Ikebana with the mass bouquet type of Europe. One must understand thoroughly decorative motifs and the furnishings of that age to interpret floral designing of a period or country. Western floral arrangement has been dependent on geometrical design and color for decoration and expression.

Plates 9, 26, 27, 28, 29 illustrate influence of Oriental design in America today. Liberties have been taken with the three segments as found in Oriental design and which are here produced to show the preference of the author, expressing his individuality in design. Flowers have been used in each case as an accent. The Oriental does not use figurines in his arrangements; however, Americans feel they add atmosphere and line in the design. They also add interest to the story that is told in the floral composition.

In Plate 26, *Oriental Grace,* a prayer table from a Buddhist Temple is the accessory needed for the feeling of Oriental influence in developing the flower arrangement. This table is about two hundred and fifty years old, and is made of aged, black lacquered wood with highlights of gold leaf. The undercoat of Chinese red lacquer escapes through the worn places on this table, muting the color. An usabata of delicate lines and proportion holds the graceful, curving Scotch broom suggestive of the three segments (heaven, man, and earth) of Oriental design. Pink floribunda roses placed in an asymmetrical triangular pattern add color and floral interest, even though they cover the nemoto. The arrangement shows the American preference for flowers while utilizing Oriental line. The figurine, that of an old man, is carved from a bamboo root, signifying the age of floral art.

74

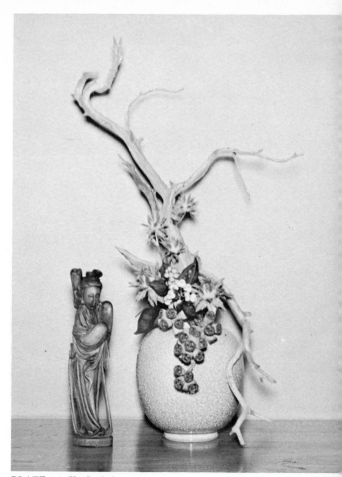

Buddhist Prayer Gong PLATE 27

PLATE 28 *Hush of Autumn*

Plate 27, *Buddhist Prayer Gong,* is an interesting development of a floral design in which an old Buddhist prayer gong is used as a container. The gong itself retains the age-old patina that antiquity alone can impart. Its base is of Chinese red lacquer with highlights of worn touches of gold. Scotch broom suggestive of the three segments of Oriental design is repositioned in a contemporary manner, but showing clearly the strength of the nemoto. Copper colored roses are used for the floral accent and color. The expression of the figurine is one of amazement; his robes repeat the colors of the container and flowers.

Plate 28, *Hush of Autumn,* expresses a quiet, dignified, mood established by the gently flowing lines of the figure. The neutral tones in the dried materials retain this quiet feeling. The materials suggest the lines of Oriental design, and the appreciation is shown of plant materials in all stages of growth.

PLATE 27
Buddhist Prayer Gong

Mysticism is created from smoke of burning incense suggested by the graceful curving lines of scotch broom. A saffron robed Buddhist priest expresses surprise at the accent of yellow roses.

PLATE 28
Hush of Autumn

Neutral tones in the dried materials suggest a quiet dignified mood, turning thoughts to Fall.

75

PLATE 29
Indo China Junk

Oriental influence is seen in this design using seasonal fruited branches with flowers in a manner simulating natural growth.

Another example of Oriental influence is shown in Plate 29, *Indo-China Junk*, using an Indo-Chinese junk for a container. The "Shin," "Soe," "Tai" lines are established by a red berried shrub, repeating the rich mahogany color of the container. Fuji chrysanthemums in a naturalistic manner are used to retain the Oriental mood. The figurine, a water buffalo with caretaker, adds atmosphere. The bamboo mat is suggestive of native materials and the reeds growing in the water of this area.

If one will bring together all of the forces that affect floral art (e.g., the nature of man, historical influences, materials, the Oriental and European influence) and keep them firmly in mind, the concept of *Free Form — Interpretive Design* can now be broken into specific elements for analysis. These elements, if used with freedom of expression, will bring rewards which no measure of material wealth can equal.

Chapter III. Principles

Chapter III

Principles

INTRODUCTION

The two terms *Principles* and *Elements* are synonymous. They are used interchangeably in this book.

> *Principle* — an essential element, constituent, or quality, especially one that produces a specific effect: as the principles of design.

> *Element* — a component, feature, or principle of something; basic part, rudiments. Irreducible parts or principles of anything concrete or abstract.

Each basic component is discussed individually; their definitions do envelop each other for one is dependent on the other. Their inter-relatedness is almost inseparable.

Design principles are fascinating as a theoretical study, but when actively applied to an arrangement, self-expression then can be one of the most rewarding of all human endeavors. Esthetic taste is expressed in design, thus enhancing the beauty of the flowers. Flowers placed in a vase without any thought of design are satisfying simply because flowers in themselves are satisfying. They are self-sufficient — an end unto themselves. However, the same flowers arranged according to *Free Form — Interpretive Design* become

78

works of creative art. The artist working with them assumes a challenge to epitomize their natural beauty to the best advantage. Their intrinsic value is inspiration.

In developing the *Free Form — Interpretive Design* floral picture, there are several important concepts that must be defined and thoroughly understood. These concepts, when diligently mastered and creatively applied, impart to an arrangement the precious elements of *Excellence* — distinction, individuality, and originality.

DISTINCTION is that quality, that "something" which sets a design apart. It is that superior or worthy quality, gained through skillful use of materials, which amplifies intrinsic characteristics, thus attracting immediate attention and giving special honor.

INDIVIDUALITY is the expression of a designer's personality. It is that quality which is immediately recognizable by his individual style, color selection, and sensitive appreciation of materials, which combine to make a design "personal."

ORIGINALITY is the reflection of creative thinking, imagination, vision, and interpretation, that incorporates distinction and individuality.

Free Form — Interpretive Design depends upon these elements, for one must be able to "see" the possibilities of design in materials. Originality is the yardstick of an open mind with vision; it urges the daring to experiment, creates the desire for something different, and strengthens the fortitude to stand firm on one's own interpretation. Materials may be commonplace, but the use the artist makes of them gives the unique effect which is definitely not a "copy".

All art forms are developed by the employment of fundamental principles which govern design. The results vary in form according to the expression of the individual.

EXPRESSION is emotion resulting in action from the urge to create — that inner desire to fulfill, caused by inspiration.

The urge to create, to act when inspiration comes, results in form of some type, e.g., poetry, painting, floral art, etc. This happens momentarily — as when hearing the crackle of crisp leaves in the Fall, the feel of a gentle breeze on the cheeks, on seeing a flower or a work of art which lingers in the subconscious mind. The creative thought may lie dormant for a long time, but when the right time or place, or combination of these presents itself, design evolves. For example, in Plate *Frontispiece* and Plate 30, the author saw this most expressive pair of sculptured hands in a display room; this impression lingered in his memory. Sculptured hands as individual objects do not generally appeal to most people, but the expression of those hands was like a portrait revealing the whole character of a person. They kept emerging from the subconscious mind, carrying their message in their expressive pose — this message of entity revealing a world in their grasp, of man's appeal to mysticism.

Shortly thereafter in the author's greenhouse this exquisite blossom (Monstera deliciosa) opened in all its glory. It expressed fulfillment, entity, the culmination of purpose. The soft, antique-ivory, white corolla encased the spadix with such love and protection that its story of life was unfolded in perfect harmony with nature. At this instant the hands seemed to embrace this blossom — design evolved. Each had similar sculptural qualities in form and texture. Color harmony was perfection in a monochromatic hue. The two were united to create fulfillment — expression — emotion — action.

The round cross-section of the black walnut tree (natural) is symbolic of the universe. Its concentric rings create earth rhythms. The white, worn pebbles rest on the earth's surface, depicting the waves of the sea. The hands rise majestically above the sea, from which all creatures emerged into space. Their cupped position reiterates earth rhythms, and appears to encircle the protective corolla of the spadix, in whose power is held the secret of life — the seed.

"Timeless" entity — this one perfect blossom is the culmination of all purpose — symbolic of man attuned to nature.

PLATE 30
Entity

"Timeless" entity — this one perfect blossom is a culmination of all purpose — symbolic of man attuned to nature.

Any new idea meets with opposition until one grows accustomed to the change. In art, each design speaks differently to the one viewing it. Emotional reaction varies as to cultural background. One who is widely read or traveled will have a more open mind: He will have many more impressions of design than one who refuses progressive ideas, new materials, or knows not what is happening in the world that affects his life. When traveling in Greece the inspiration on seeing the magnificent ruins of Melos, Parnassus, and Athens may so fire a person's imagination that all history races through conscious thought. It is no great wonder that Grecian culture revitalizes new civilizations periodically. Beauty of form and perfection of design always endure regardless of age. Plate 1.

Those whom tradition holds in its hypnotic power and who resist change will prefer period or conventional designs as in Plates 40, 46, and 62. Change takes effort — it means study and generally is refused unless met by a progressive, receptive attitude. When designing, one may recall the joys of traveling for inspiration. He may remember a scene, an interesting figurine or an unusual flower, which stimulates the imagination, and causes ideas to run rampant.

The Orient holds an allure for the author that no other part of the world can equal. He experienced this inspiration when finding the statuette of Indonesia. In Plate 31, *Bali,* a whole story is brought to mind — snake charming, court dances, brilliant blossoms of the tropics, the quiet of a moonlit night where mystery of the Orient and the South Seas prevails. The tall, boat-shaped leaves of the tropical palms, (Molineria recurvata), are suggestive of the temple spires of Indonesia which pierce the skyline. The vertical lines of the ribs in the foliage give emphasis and rhythm, accenting the stylized figurine. She characterizes the people of this country as they pause before their temples. The coiled, wooden gnarl represents the cobra which is associated with this region. It is motionless as though charmed by mystical notes vibrating from the brilliant red anthurium.

PLATE 31
Bali

Tall, boat-shaped leaves of the tropical palm represent temple spires of Indonesia which pierce the sky. The stylized figure characterizes the people poised before their temples. A coiled wooden gnarl represents the cobra associated with this region. It is motionless as though charmed by the mystic notes vibrating from the brilliant red anthurium.

82

COMPOSITION

Composition and harmony are closely related and are often thought of in conjunction with each other. Both terms are abstract, each has a varying connotation to the individual. Composition is the selection and subsequent grouping of components to create a pattern (design). All parts must be selected to complete a single idea or theme and be compatible with their environs. Discordant material and unrelated accessories should be omitted. If objects do not add materially to an idea being expressed, they should be ruthlessly discarded regardless of their intrinsic value. Each component should contribute its full value to the completed whole.

An arrangement of flowers in the container may fulfill all the requirements of good design within itself. However, should it not be compatible with its setting or blend with the decor of the room, it will be unsatisfactory because unity is lost. Its purpose as a decorative piece will be discordant. The word "suitability" is important and must be considered. With the rapid changes in culture, one's appreciation changes with the times. Acceptance of new combinations influences one's decisions as to suitability. Personal preference as to "good taste" — which means the right time, the right place, and the right purpose, can only answer this question of harmonious composition. For festive occasions, one may decorate with designs not compatible with the interior of the home, e.g., Christmas, Halloween, special parties, etc. The design here gives the theme of the affair. But in designing a decorative piece for the home, or for entering in flower show competition, one must unify the composition to complete the whole scheme or follow the rules of the show schedule.

Composition need not be restricted to definite periods or any one category. It gains distinction by its originality in selection of materials and their skillful blending. This is best illustrated for interior decor in combining foreign influence with traditional and modern furniture and with accessories to create a harmonious setting.

Plate 32, *Composition — Author's Home,* is a view of the living room. The contemporary painting dominates the atmosphere of the room and governs the entire composition of the interior design. There is freedom, however, in what this painting allows in expression. It is Post-Impressionistic in technique and speaks of Fauvism in the daring choice of color, yet there is a suggestion of tradition in the composition within itself. This picture, though contemporary, is "at home" and in perfect harmony with its somewhat traditional setting. The warm tone of the background color is a welcome note that glows. The pewter pitcher holding the artichoke leaves is friendly in its commonplace design, and is so painted that it appears to be free of the background, which is suggested by the perspective lines giving depth. The leaves, a continuation of the handle, flow naturally into the fruit and vegetable grouping. Line created by the grapes, and continued into the peppers, returns the eye to complete the visual motion. Rhythm and transition are so carefully handled by the artist one is entranced. The background wall and draperies of the room are a neutral off-white color. The music cabinet was designed and made by the author to fit this room. It is made of black walnut from specially selected trees with wood grain matched in the finished design.

The flower arrangement shows the Oriental influence of his world tour. The container, an usabata some 250 years old, has a base which suggests the ocean waves in the gently rolling ribbons of bronze with the whitecaps portrayed in the curly filigree fingers. The whitecaps pick up the texture of the artichoke leaves in the painting. The gold artichoke blossoms, in true classical Japanese Ikenobo design, are in harmony with the usabata and unite with their own foliage in the painting. The form of the artichoke is reminiscent of the lotus blossom in the Buddhist temples of the Orient. The lyrical rhythm created by the one strelitzia leaf adds force by picking up the flow of line in the picture, and carrying the eye into the permanent floral design and on down through the "one" stem (nemoto) and stem of the container. The eye naturally moves to the round vase whose color is a repetition of the dominant color of the main background of the picture, and adds emphasis to the round forms in the picture that are somewhat subordinate. These round vegetables now have increased value and relationship to the whole. The French antique chair, upholstered in gold, adds rhythm with its beautiful curved back that blends with the design of the cabinet. The contemporary lounge chair blends in color and modern feeling with the painting. Here is the definite influence of a contemporary painting, traditional in composition, accented with an Oriental flower arrangement, carrying much symbolism and reflection of travel, with a personally designed cabinet and with chairs of other periods so perfectly blended that the whole composition is in perfect harmony. This composition is unified by color, texture, rhythmic line, and transition of periods.

Composition is the one element that most fulfills or satisfies the urge for artistic expressions. Composition in design may tell a story (Plate 33), it may express a mood (Plate 34), recall a scene (Plate 35), or may reflect pure *Free-Form* design (Plate 36), whether for self-expression or for its own sake.

Composition In A Story

It has been said that the Indians in Central America who worshipped the birds were continually at war with those who used the winged serpent as a symbol of strength and virility. They exterminated their race by continuous wars. Plate 33, *An Allegorical Tale*, tells this story in abstract form. The embryo palm branch is representative of the sacred quetzal bird with feathers flushed, defying the feathered serpent (driftwood) who has coiled around orange marigold blossoms. The color orange has come to be symbolic of the Soul in purgatory. Since this flower blossoms in the Fall, the time of All Saints' Day, natives use the petals of this flower to scatter down the

PLATE 32
Composition— Author's Home

Perfect harmony is created in the unique combination of a dominating Post-Impressionistic oil painting with an Oriental arrangement and period furniture. This composition shows rhythm transition of foreign influence, and historical to contemporary periods carefully combined.

86

PLATE 33

An Allegorical Tale

A story is told in abstract form with the embryo palm representing the sacred quetzal bird defying the serpent coiled around orange marigold blossoms. Orange color is symbolic of the Soul in purgatory and is used in Indian religious rituals when praying for their departed ones. Tritoma blossoms are in flight toward heaven's freedom.

aisle of the cathedral and on the altar when praying for the departed ones.

The quetzal is a shy, brilliantly colored bird of Central America. The crested head and neck feathers are usually brilliant green and the lower part of the body is red with long streaming iridescent tail feathers. In Guatemala this bird is loved to the point of reverence. Their monetary system is based on the Quetzales named in honor of this bird.

In Mexico the feathered serpent appears on their national flag. The serpent appears to have mastery over this symbolic flower. The tritoma, often called shooting star, an embryo palm representing the bird, are symbolic of ethereal quality. They are in flight toward Heaven.

88

PLATE 35
Prairie Solitude — A Scene

The characteristic pose of the Brahman bull in its environmental setting of the Southwest recalls a familiar scene. Each piece of floral material lends its full support in expressing the theme. This weathered, black branch of live oak, forced by the prevailing winds of the prairie to grow in this distorted manner, creates directiontal motion which adds realism to the spirit of the theme.

It is covered with blotches of gray lichen, repeating the colors of the animal. The prickly pear cactus, (Opuntia streptacantha), with its purplish red fruit adds an interesting color note. Red cedar foliage represents the green range; its stubbiness is due to the cattle's continuous grazing on the tender new growth. This scenic picture needs no flowers; they are suggested by the prickly pear fruit. Familiarity of the area brings to mind the fields of spring flowers covering the prairies.

PLATE 34
Serenity — Mood

Expresses a mood. The large, clear crystal hurricane globe encloses the madonna and sets it apart from the surroundings. The carnations in crescent design are suggestive of an ethereal body — the new moon. Dark red roses express emotion of love and add color contrast. During Easter and Christmas holiday seasons an ethereal theme is created, setting the mood for worshipping.

89

Again a mood reflecting tranquility and repose is portrayed in Plate 59, *Tranquility*. The gently curved cedar and resting gazelle express harmony with nature. This tranquil quality is produced by the predominantly horizontal line of the cedar tree trunk and diminished by the agave leaf which terminates in infinity. The figurine, gazelle at rest, emphasizes the feeling of repose. The foliage is spiral ginger, (Costus speciosus), repeating the curves of the cedar. Day lilies are selected for color and fleeting moments of time.

Composition for Pure Design

For pure design (*Free Form — Interpretive Design*) a stylized figurine, Plate 36, *Modern Madonna*, suggests the pattern of a floral arrangement. In this picture the accessory is not used as a religious symbol, but is one of contemporary design used for decorative motif only. The ancient Chinese stirrup has been inverted and stylized as a container, using rectangular supports in contrast to the curves. The selection of flame ginger, (Alpinia purpurata), is perfect in petal form and line to complement the featured work of art. Each petal repeats the shape of the hands. The flowers are arranged in abstract line to follow the body lines of the figurine and they also add strong color contrast. The aspidistra foliage again adds emphasis to the shape of the hands, although they are spaced separately as seen in cubism. The solid leaf gives the feeling of strength. This floral material is placed so as to continue the line down through the support of the container. The turn of the madonna's head is a repetition of the position of the top ginger blossom. This composition expresses pure design which is free of geometric restrictions.

PLATE 36
Modern Madonna

This beautifully carved figurine suggests the floral pattern. It is not used as a religious symbol but one of contemporary form as a decorative motif. The flame ginger blossoms used in abstract line, rise majestically, re-creating the flow of the body lines of the figurine.

90

HARMONY

Harmony expresses the relationship between components chosen. Harmony is unity — it creates impression. It is sometimes difficult to understand for it is an abstract term varying with personal taste. This principle brings elements together, thus creating the impression of completeness. This combination of composition and harmony forms a pleasing concordant whole where unity is immediately obvious. A work within itself may have all the principles well executed, but may fail in the final results because of its placement. In dealing with intangibles, appreciation and personal preference may be the deciding factors in many cases.

Generally most flowers can be combined harmoniously; however, the associational attributes often are unfavorable. For example: zinnias, sweet peas, roses, and marigolds grow together in the garden, but they are not compatible companions in most floral arrangements. Rough texture is associated with zinnias and marigolds, and a fine texture with roses and sweet peas. A grouping of zinnias and sweet peas would not blend, nor would the zinnias feel at home in a cut-glass or fine textured china whereas sweet peas would be lovely. It is interesting to note, however, that some flowers will be harmonious with many varied materials. For example: Roses are versatile; they can be happy in the finest of containers or content in rough earthenware jugs.

Fast social and scientific advances are changing one's concepts of harmonious units. Tradition is rapidly being broken. This change is seen in religious rituals, attitudes toward social activities, architecture, as well as in interior decor which mixes custom and art of many countries. In *Free Form — Interpretive Design*, there is no need to hold to a definite period in the selection of materials.

92

Much contemporary art blends harmoniously with older designs; periods can be mixed in perfect harmony. The design in Plate 10, *Egypt*, contemporary in appearance, was inspired by hieroglyphics in the tombs of the Pharaohs. Its etched form appears to have been created for today's homes. The Grecian Horse (Plate 1), although sculptured in 470 B. C., is beautifully proportioned reflecting a spatial quality to our "modern" eye, and would enhance any contemporary setting.

One of the definitions of design states that "design is the inter-relatedness, psychological effects of materials, their associational value, shape, color, and space so arranged that a pleasing whole is obtained." So it is with harmony; this definition is explanatory. In reviewing the various subjects of composition — as a mood, a story, a scene, a design for pure design's sake, etc. — each must be developed with suitable material, and the final arrangement in accord with its setting to result in harmony. It is that quality of being one in spirit, sentiment, mood, theme, and purpose which completes the whole.

In Plate 37, *Harmony*, an excellent example of harmony was achieved by expressing the purpose for which the flower arrangement was made, by the selection of materials, container, and perfect blending of floral design with room decor. The occasion was the opening of a new bank building and this arrangement was featured in the board of directors' room. An antique balance scales was selected to give the theme of the design, suggesting the weighing of decisions by the members. Fruitful action is represented by the heavier, lower side of the scales, showing an abundance of fruit and flowers. Miniature pineapples and grapes are covered with mother-of-pearl to complement the texture of the white, raw silk draperies. White birds-of-paradise, (Strelitzia nicholai), whose black boat-shaped corollas contrast in form and color, add an exotic note. The higher, opposite side of the scales holds rare eremurus (foxtail) lilies from Persia whose spike form represents the divergence of opinions and personalities of the directors. The beautiful gold color and exquisite texture of both lilies and draperies are in perfect harmony. Ti foliage, (Cordyline terminalis), painted black, and contrasting white anthurium are combined with lilies to repeat the surface quality of the leather upholstered furniture. The arrangement is in a large, hand-wrought tray from the Middle East. The imported flora and tray suggest business with foreign countries.

Harmony is one of the important principles of design which pleases the esthetic taste. It is inter-dependent with composition.

PLATE 37
Harmony

Purpose and personality are expressed in this design for a Board of Directors' room, perfectly blending with the decor. An antique balance scale is selected to suggest the weighing of the decisions of the members. Gold colored eremurus lilies express the divergence of opinion and the lower side of the scales showing abundance of fruit and flowers represents fruitful action. White anthurium and painted fruit accent the draperies.

94

PLATE 38
The Pulque Jug

A strong focal point is established by the agave plant and reinforced by the radiating lines of the strelitzia flowers.

FOCAL POINT

In life we have an aim — a purpose to which we direct effort. It may be found in the guidance of our children, or a goal we wish to achieve in business. In either case this is a focus towards which we strive. So it is with any creative project we undertake.

In all forms of art this important principle is the governing factor, whether it be in traditional or contemporary design, it is the focus — the aim to which the artist directs attention. In writing, e.g., poetry, it is the message or thought that is the ultimate aim; in mystery stories it is the development of the events leading to the climax.

In traditional painting there is one central feature most prominent. However, in some modern paintings the focus is not apparent. There may seem to be just blotches of paint on canvas with no definite focus or story to tell, but the artist's intention is on color, letting the imagination roam. Regardless of subject, the artist is directing our attention to that one point, the aim, or intent — the focus, a center of interest.

In traditional flower arrangement the focal point is the point of origin or convergence to which the eye is drawn by virtue of the perspective in geometrical pattern (design). It is almost a defined "bull's-eye" where a single design element is emphasized by its characteristics and by arrangement of support elements so that they converge. This spot dominates the composition. This illusion can be created only by the inherent characteristics of the design element. Dominance is synonymous with emphasis — focus. The term dominance is discussed later as a separate subject.

Floral art, in the years preceding the free form movement, had a feature to which all others were subordinated. The lesser ones were used to emphasize this feature and lead the eye to it by development of line or transition of materials and color. As Western flower arrangement developed, rules governed which demanded the definition of this area. The strongest color or the most fully developed blossom was used at this well defined focal point, or bull's-eye.

In Plate 38, *The Pulque Jug*, each line of floral material converges at the base of the Guatemalan Indian and culminates with the agave plant which is used at the focal point. The thick, thorny, radiating leaves of the agave plant tie in each line to their base, giving stronger emphasis to this point. The theme developed in this picture tends to accent the focal point: The native woman is carrying a pulque jug, suggesting the gathering of agave plant juices from which pulque is made. The strong converging lines of the strelitzia flowers reinforce this point.

The focus in the floral pattern of Plate 39, *Parrot Tulips*, is the opened tulip which is accented by the simulated bow tied with tulip foliage. Directional lines developed by the placement of the bells-of-Ireland and semi-opened parrot tulips accentuate this defined focus. Container, texture, and floral material complement each other harmoniously. The design of the beaded portion of the container emphasizes the focus by leading the eye to the one central blossom.

Fig. 2
A well defined focal point. See photos 38-39.

Fig. 3
Cross hatching of stems cause confusion.

97

Thus in geometrical pattern, the focal point is clearly defined. The main axis of a design runs through this focus, and balance is governed by the division of materials. The more fully developed blossoms, the greatest weight, and the most vivid tonal values, are placed to give importance to the focus which must be at a logical point governed by the design. In symmetrical design (formal) it is centered, in asymmetrical design (informal) it is toward the high side of the arrangement. Cross-hatching of stems confuses focal point development, as does the placing of stems upright across the container like soldiers marching in a line; the stems do not converge at any particular place; the design appears to fall apart. Even though the stems do not reach the exact point of focus, their lines, if continued, should converge at this terminus.

Generally when a figurine is used within the design, it is placed at the focus. In Plate 40, *Symbolic Numbers,* the figurine is perfectly at home in its setting, the center of interest, dominating the arrangement. Lines of all flowers and foliage flow toward the center of interest, adding strength. The use of three rubber plant leaves, five gladioli, seven tulips, nine tulip leaves (3-5-7-9), is representative of the mystical numbers. In the pyramidal arrangement of pale yellow gladioli, the buds suggest the curved fingers of Oriental dancers and emphasize the rhythmic sway found in the figurine. The dark foliage of the rubber plant, (Ficus elastica), adds background to the center of interest; lemon yellow tulips in the "S" curve formation reiterate the rhythmic motion of the design. Tulip foliage radiates at the base, completing the radiating points of the gladioli.

In Plate 41, *Vertical Rhythm,* the figurine dominates the entire composition and is the center of focus. The units in this case are subordinate to the accessory which, by form and contrast, is the outstanding feature. The rhythmic movement created by lines of this

PLATE 40
Symbolic Numbers

The Oriental figurine placed against the dark green background is the focus of the pyramidal floral arrangement. The use of three rubber plant leaves, 5 gladioli, seven tulips, nine tulip leaves (3-5-7-9) is representative of the mystical numbers.

figurine is strengthened by the flame ginger that seems to caress the madonna. The tall, parallel ribbed palm leaves, (Molineria recurvata), in the background lend support to the motion created by the upward movement of the original lines. The three leaves are symbolic of temple spires that pierce the skyline of Indo China and India.

Free Form — Interpretive Design presents an entirely different concept of focus. This principle is still one of the most vital principles but it is not the set bull's-eye concept used in geometric design. Space assumes new importance. Its relationship to the whole composition coordinates in harmonious balance units which may appear to be separate and unites them by inter-relatedness of pure design elements.

In Plate 1, *Grecian Horse*, the component parts are inter-related by juxtaposition of form, each repeating the other's sculptural qualities. The relation of units is in complete harmony without actual physical ties. There are no converging lines to one point.

In Plate 36, *Modern Madonna*, the aspiring rhythm, created through vertical parallel lines of madonna and flame ginger, harmonizes the composition. The focus is centered on pure design.

The ceramic ribbons in Plate 55, *Motion in Space*, cut space, thus creating beauty in motion. The focus is on the spatial quality of design. The lines are united but do not define a central focus, nor does one opened blossom or brilliant color define a focal point.

This new concept first appeared in painting when it broke with tradition about the mid-19th century and developed through the various stages of "isms," finally reaching its peak with Picasso. His paintings, Cubist in style, show parts of objects in rectangular or triangular forms that seem unrelated as far as representation of full subject matter is concerned. They appear disconnected, though these pieces, so to speak, are bits of subject matter suggesting the whole composition. The focus is on the subject told by the segments. In American floral design we have not gone that far in presenting

100

PLATE 41

Vertical Rhythm

Rhythmic movement created by lines of the sculptured figurine is strengthened by flame ginger blossoms which seem to caress the madonna. The background foliage of tall, parallel-ribbed palm leaves supports the upward movement.

the new concept of focus in our arrangements, but we have deviated far from the established rule concerning this principle, the focal point, or the center of interest.

Free Form design has freed itself of the restrictive requirements of vanishing point perspective where all lines converge to the one dominant feature. This new concept of focus may be found in pure design itself, where form fulfills appreciation of design. Let us digress for a minute and reconsider Japanese floral design — it has no center of interest as compared to conventional Occidental design. The Japanese interest is to project the personality, the spiritual, physical, and symbolic value of the material suggesting the region and season of the countryside. If they have a focal point (focus) it definitely is in symbolism.

101

DOMINANCE

Dominance is synonymous with emphasis. It is the leading character in the play of materials within the arrangement, and in placement of the arrangement in its setting. Dominance is the development of a center of interest in conventional designs or it is the development of a theme or mood in *Free Form — Interpretive Design*. Dominance prevents conflict. It subordinates lesser units to the main idea. It is natural for the materials in an arrangement to have a starting point which is the logical place of dominance, the point to which the eye is first attracted. This center of interest is vital to geometric patterns, but in *Free Form — Interpretive Design* it becomes less important because the theme or mood is often the focus itself. Lines converge toward a point or points, but the area is not definitely established as in a geometric design. Plate 31, *Bali,* has perfect focus in the story it tells. Each unit is individual and blends with the whole. The four units, Bali figurine, anthurium, leaves, and curled driftwood, appear to have equal value and importance; no one unit dominates. The idea conjured in the imagination suffices to fill the requirements of dominance. Again in Plate 71, *Surrealism — Space Man,* there is no bull's-eye focus, but elements are closely related and unify the composition. The focus is on pure design in abstract. In the two Plates, 31 and 71 mentioned above, both designs are stripped of all non-essentials and each detail adds full value to the design.

The stylized ceramic bird, by H. Clante of Denmark, Plate 42, *Danish Modern Hen,* so dominates its surroundings that the center of interest is on the container. The strelitzia and foliage become subordinate and are an accent foil for the container. Lines of the design are suggested and controlled by the ceramic artwork. The material is sympathetic and blends so perfectly with the container that it is hard to picture one without the other. Unity in line, texture, and design, in both container and floral arrangement, is so compatible that dominance is achieved. (Plates 2, 3, and 4).

102

PLATE 42
Danish Modern Hen

The container so dominates it environment that it becomes the center of interest and with mate rials so sympathetic, perfect i form and line, it is hard to pic ture one without the other.

BALANCE AND PROPORTION

Balance and proportion are in most cases interdependent, as are composition and harmony. Balance is equilibrium. Balance is achieved by the division of materials by visual or actual weight to either side of a central axis, center of gravity. Proportion is the comparative relationship between individual parts of a composition in size and quantity in harmonious balance. These two terms are used interchangeably in many instances. In this writing balance refers to the relationship of units within the individual design. Proportion encompasses the environs in addition to the units of the design. Proportion is referred to as scale when comparing the arrangement with its placement.

Formal balance is man made and recognizable on sight. Asymmetrical balance is natural and somewhat abstract. An accomplished ballet dancer may be motionless on points, but the weight is so distributed that a feeling of equilibrium is produced; grace and beauty results. The Leaning Tower of Pisa is balanced by weight in relation to the center of gravity, but it does not have visual balance; therefore, an awed, disturbed feeling is produced. An arrangement so constructed would give the beholder an uneasy feeling. When not looking at the arrangement, the subconscious mind would be disturbed by faulty balance.

Plate 43, *Dynamic Equilibrium,* similar to the Leaning Tower of Pisa, shows a strong line with terrific force shooting up to the right. However, this line of strelitzia, accentuated with desert spoons, is counterbalanced with the heavy, compact, dark red celosia at its base. The celosia is similar to a block of concrete giving stability and visual balance through its dynamic force. The solid base of the container adds to this firmness.

104

PLATE 43
Dynamic Equilibrium

This unusual arrangement, similar to the Leaning Tower of Pisa, presents balance through novel construction. Continuation of the line on one side of the container by the strelitzia is counterbalanced with a heavy, compact, dark red celosia mass to the other side giving stability and balance.

Correct balance results in a feeling of stability and security. It is achieved in two ways:

1. *Mechanical or structural balance is gained by the proper placement of main stems forming design or pattern. These materials establish the skeletal pattern of the desired composition. This may be referred to as the blueprint or skeleton.*

>   A. *Symmetrical—formal, perfect, man made equilateral (Plate 46)*

>   B. *Asymmetrical (Occult) — informal, natural (Plate 47)*

2. *Visual balance is achieved by the proper use of color and placement in sequence of related sizes of materials (Plate 53) in conjunction with structural balance.*

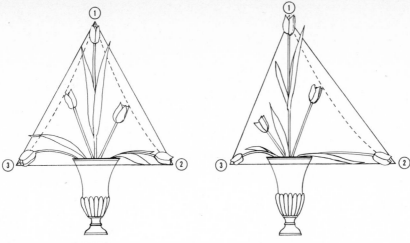

Fig. 4
Formal balance, perfect symmetry.

Fig. 5
Informal, natural balance, asymmetry.

Symmetrical Balance is characterized by perfect symmetry. The central stem giving the height of the arrangement is always placed first. It is directly over the "frog" which is positoned in the center of the container. This axis bisects the composition. It establishes the center axis from which develops the corresponding side arms; both are equal in length and usually similar in kind. These three elements established, the symmetrical triangle is thus formed. They are the structural foundation of the design. No material crosses the imaginary lines. Should these lines be crossed, a fan-shaped arrangement is approached. A curved line is formed by the material from the apex of the center line to the points at either side. This curved line adds grace and beauty, taking less flowers and producing a greater image. Generally, objects on one side are matched with those on the other. Wedding decorations, dining room table centerpieces and arrangements for teas and receptions are usually planned in formal balance.

Seldom is formal balance seen in natural growing plants. Some conifers, e.g., Colorado blue spruce and Norfolk Island pine, are nearly formal in natural growth. Man, due to his instinct to organize, uses this pattern for authority and formality.

Formal balance is portrayed in Plate 46, *Cherub, with Orchids,* showing a bilateral triangular arrangement. The central axis, running through the cherub's leg and arm, establishes this line through the arrangement, dividing the floral material into two seg-

PLATE 44
Formal Tea

This Empire epergne with a silver plateau holds a symmetrical triangular design of spring flowers. Formality is further heightened by the pair of candelabra.

PLATE 45
Floral Fountain

Formal balance is clearly defined in the tiered cone shaped arrangement of the white chrysanthemum constructed to be viewed from all sides. It is made more prominent by the footed elevation of the container.

PLATE 46
Cherub With Orchids

Formal bilateral, triangular balance showing grace and beauty is portrayed in this arrangement. The delicate youthful beauty of the cherub is complemented by the delicate lines of the flowers.

106

PLATE 44 *Formal Tea*

Floral Fountain PLATE 45

Cherub With Orchids PLATE 46

ments. The orchids in the upper portion are to the left of this axis, while those blossoms on the lower side are to the right, thus creating a feeling of good visual balance, but the design is without absolute symmetry thereby avoiding monotony. This treatment creates a curved line that is gentle and relaxing, relieving the stiffness of formality.

In Plate 44, *Formal Tea*, the Empire epergne with a silver plateau for a base holds the symmetrical triangular design for a formal occasion. This is an excellent illustration of structural man made balance. The Empire period in history greatly influenced interior decor and dress styles. Strength and grandeur of the Napoleonic invasions are expressed in the pyramidal floral pattern and the decorative motif, winged lions (griffins), on the standard of the epergne.

Perfect symmetry or formal balance may also be obtained in the shape of the cone. It does not have the side extensions, but we do have perfect symmetry and balance. In Plate 45, *Floral Fountain*, formality in design is illustrated in the pyramidal arrangement which has perfect symmetry. The tiered, white chrysanthemum formation is alternated with silver strips of palm sheaths, each circling over a silver teasel burr. The cone is suggestive of the Byzantine and Persian periods. Plate 14 illustrates the same basic design.

In *Asymmetrical Balance*, a high vertical line appears on one side and is counterbalanced on the other by a low horizontal line. Good balance is achieved without perfect symmetry. Equilibrium is produced by careful distribution of quantities to either side of the central axis. Asymmetrical balance is natural and relaxing. In America one's eyes are trained to accept the left to right movement. A printed page is read from the upper left, and ending at the lower right; clocks move left to right (clockwise); cars are driven from the left side, etc. Since this movement is familiar arrangements are most pleasing when done in this manner.

108

This interesting, though simple, arrangement, of orchid colored Fuji chrysanthemums is done in an asymmetrical manner, Plate 47, *Fuji and Caladiums.* It is graceful and informal. The pink caladium foliage is more prominent on the left side to counterbalance the extra flowers on the right, yet there is perfect visual balance. The foliage has character, shows weight, but does not compete with the flowers. The two contrast in texture and surface; the caladium is solid and broad while the Fuji chrysanthemums have a fragile, delicate appearance. Here is good, asymmetrical design, giving visual balance with an interesting play of texture. The bowl is similar to the rice bowls used in Japan.

PLATE 47
Fuji and Caladiums

Pink Fuji chrysanthemums with pink caladium foliage arranged in a graceful informal asymmetrical design also present near-perfect visual balance.

However, this pattern is altered when the background dictates otherwise, as in Plate 48 where the design pattern conforms to the staircase. The *Asymmetrical* triangular pattern is immediately noticeable in the background wall area.

PLATE 48

In Plate 48, flowers and fruit form the floral pattern conforming to the triangle set by the line of the staircase and the top of the cabinet. The stock blossoms give the proportion and design. The upper flower and container continue the vertical line of the cabinet and staircase. The lower blossom carries the eye toward the vase and candles. Interest in accessories counterbalances the floral design. This composition has excellent visual asymmetrical balance.

A pair of asymmetrical arrangements designed for a mantel may be placed to frame a picture or mirror, thus producing formal balance in the composition as a whole, Plate 49. These arrangements will accent the corners of the frame.

Plate 50 shows two arrangements used in opposite direction. The vertical lines of the frame become dominant. The two asymmetrical arrangements give perfect symmetry. It is interesting to use arrangements in pairs to give formal balance. For dinner parties or formal receptions, a candelabrum or statuette may be used in the center of the table, flanked with an arrangement to either side. The arrangements shown can be used to good advantage in this manner. As a point of interest for perfect balance, picture the two arrangements in Plate 49 or 50 in weighing scales. An excellent example of formal balance would be produced. In Plate 53 there is equal balance but the two arrangements are not similar.

Visual Balance is gained by the selection of correct sizes of materials, and uses of color, texture, etc. The eye unconsciously considers these related elements. A pound of feathers and a pound of lead have equal weight and balance (mechanical), however, they do not have visual balance. They are out of proportion in comparison to each other in size. This comparison is true in flower arrangement when combining the large, ball shaped chrysanthemum with the small button or daisy pompon flower. Transition of size and visual balance are lacking.

The darker colors appear heavier and generally should be used low. If the heavy color appears in the smaller, finer textured flower, and the lighter color in the larger mass forms, then color placement will be reversed, since color is less demanding than size. Mass and size determine visual balance in this instance to offset the color positions.

112

PLATE 51
Sea Horse

Visual weight in the focal area is obtained by reflexing the outer petals of the two tulip blossoms. Importance is gained by the increased size.

The individual flower composition — its petal arrangement — produces visual balance. A composite flower with many petals heavily set on the stem will have greater weight than a flower of the same variety with delicate petals gracefully attached to the stem. For example: The chrysanthemums, the Fuji variety, Plate 25, have much less visual weight than the incurved petal "China" type. Both are similar, yet the petal arrangement changes the weight. The ball and daisy type chrysanthemums are different in appearance.

Another excellent way of obtaining visual weight is to reflex the outer petals of the flower. A tulip, peony, or rose gains weight and importance by this treatment. In Plate 51, *Sea Horse*, the reflexed tulips gain importance by the increased size. Carnations are usually equal in size, but by reflexing the calyx we get an interesting variation. To gain visual weight, without addition of more flowers, a simulated foliage bow may be used, Plate 39, *Parrot Tulips*.

113

PLATE 52
Oriental Occult Balance

This Oriental goddess has much weight through intrinsic value and by juxtaposition is able to give excellent occult and visual balance to the composition. Delicate curving tracery in the flowers is accentuated by the graceful curves of the figurine. A Far Eastern mood is suggested by the flowers and is climaxed by the flower goddess.

To obtain visual balance, sometimes an accessory may be needed. In Plate 52, *Oriental Occult Balance*, an example of occult or visual balance is illustrated. The Oriental goddess figurine, though smaller in size, has much weight through intrinsic value and material. It gains visual weight and interest value by its subject matter, form, and texture and is able to counterbalance the grouping of blossoms in the crystal container. The curves in the tritomas repeat the lines of the figurine in the opposite direction. Chartreuse Fuji chrysanthemums bisect the composition, thereby visually dividing the structural pattern in two segments. Texture and associational value of materials, in addition to application of the principles of design, complete the visual balance in this unusual composition. Hold a sheet of paper over the figurine and notice how the design becomes unbalanced almost to the point of looking as though it will turn over. Had the figurine been placed close to the container the composition would be off balance also. Here is a good example of correct distance and space relationship for perfect balance. This illustrates occult balance — that which is seen and felt without the actual balance in weight or symmetry.

In Plate 53, *Weight of Harvest*, the central standard of the brass antique scales holds weighing pans in perfect balance; even though materials vary in quantity, each side weighs an equal amount. Equilibrium is obtained through the use of two asymmetrical arrangements. Although the arrangement in each pan has the same equal weight, the informality expressed in the floral pattern relieves this arrangement of what seems to be perfect balance. In this composition there is *perfect balance* from equal weight, *asymmetrical balance* in each weighing pan developed by the informal floral pattern, and *visual balance* in the transition of materials.

Visual Balance — In the hands of an artist, liberties are freely taken with materials to create emphasis and still maintain good proportion and balance in chosen structural pattern. Vertical arrangements may grossly exceed the $1\frac{1}{2}$:1 ratio measurement. The pattern then becomes dramatic; it gives the feeling of an exclamation point where weight flows directly down the center line giving it stability as in Plate 54, *The Cookie Jar,* and Plate 56, *An Etruscan Chalice.* In The Cookie Jar, spiraling sansevieria foliage with dried mullein seed pods are more than three times the height of the container and form the vertical line-pattern, greatly exceeding the proportions of established good rule and still satisfy visual balance. Lotus pods give weight and interest at the focus and tie in the sprays of greenish-brown cymbidium orchids. This container is a heavy, hand-blown, green glass jar made by blowing glass into a crockery jug. The jug was then broken leaving the formed container.

Consider carefully the texture of both plants and containers before combining them. Texture plays an important part in creating an appearance of proper balance. Only practice in designing will develop visual skill so that it will be obvious to the eye whether the container has the weight and stability to carry a large arrangement, or whether it is light and requires the use of graceful, airy flowers and foliage. Thin, fragile containers seem lost with a massive arrangement of flowers. Heavy, earthenware containers holding delicate flowers or sprays of flowers would lack proportion and visual balance. Fine china and crystal hold a designer to the $1\frac{1}{2}$:1 measurement; but coarse, textured containers such as pottery or wrought-iron allow greater freedom. The addition of a base will permit greater height in the arrangement to offset the problem of balance.

PLATE 54
The Cookie Jar

This composition has masculine dignity, grossly exceeding the accepted measurements—like an exclamation point. Its severe restricted line is dramatic.

117

PROPORTION

Proportion is closely related to balance and compares the relationship of the units of a composition to each other in size, quantity, and setting (environment). Proportion is often referred to as scale when applied to the placement of an arrangement.

From the Japanese, American flower arrangers have learned that proportion will be pleasing if materials are approximately $1\frac{1}{2}$ times the container's height if it is tall, or $1\frac{1}{2}$ times its width if it is low. A low container is one in which the width exceeds the height. A tall container's height exceeds its width. This $1\frac{1}{2}$:1 ratio has proven invaluable and has been established through constant use and experimentation over hundreds of years in all types of art. It may be used with safety. When a base is used under the container it is considered a portion of the container and is counted in the over-all measurements. When using line flowers or linear foliage, the buds of the line flowers and the tips of the foliage are not counted in measurements. When measuring mass-type flowers or other similar materials such as dried seed pods, cones, etc., there are no buds to be counted, since these flowers grow singly on a stem.

When making an arrangement using closed buds or slender material of mass and form flowers, the proportion may be exceeded since this measurement principle is based on visual quantity or weight. The portion of the stem in the container is not counted. The measurement ratio may be exceeded where plant materials are graceful and comparatively light in form (flowering tree branches) and the container is sturdy or gives the impression of weight. If the flower arrangements are less than $1\frac{1}{2}$ times the container's measurements, the container then will tend to dominate or "swallow" the plant materials. With floating arrangements, no more than $\frac{1}{2}$ to $\frac{1}{3}$ of the water area should be used for plants and the remainder left open. The water surface adds interest.

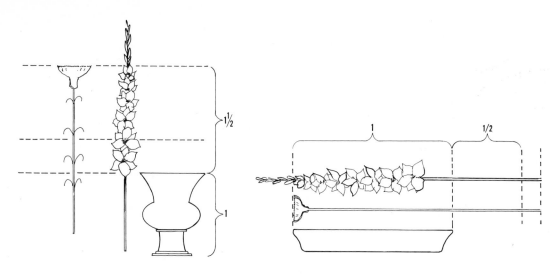

Fig. 6
*Correct proportion — measuring
a tall container.*

Fig. 7
*Correct proportion — measuring
a low container.*

The *scale* of an arrangement is governed by the furnishings of a room in which it is to be placed. A heavy, oak dining table in a room with paneled walls needs an arrangement of strength and massiveness. Fragile materials would be lost. A room decorated in fragile French style, such as Rococo, with delicate decor of flowing lines and soft pastel colors, is complemented by an arrangement of similar flower materials, Plate 18, *The Three Graces*. But in a contemporary home which is open, well-lighted, and functional, flowers must be tailored to the demands of the time.

To determine the proportion (scale) of an arrangement for a dining room table, there are two important factors to consider: First, the number of guests and second, where the dinner is to be given. When arranging for a home, the size of the dining room, the table, and the number of guests to be seated will determine the length of the arrangement. The greater the number of guests, the longer the design can be. The height of the arrangement should not exceed approximately 14 inches at its highest point, measured from the table level (not counting the length of the buds when using line flowers or unopened buds of mass and form flowers). This height

119

assures clear vision so that guests will not have to play "peek-a-boo" when talking with others across the table. The manner of serving, whether family style or formal plates, will determine the number of dishes on the table and may limit the spread of the arrangement. For speakers' tables, buffets, standing teas, and other formal affairs, the arrangements may be as tall as the proportion of the room will permit, Plate 44.

A country club or night club table arrangement is governed by the same taste used in a home arrangement, but chair spacing is more important. The night club seats people very close together and at small tables 24 to 30 inches wide. These tables are also placed as close to each other as guest circulation will allow. Here flower arrangements must be low and compact for conversation and freedom of movement. In a country club or exclusive town club larger tables and wider spacing allow expansion of a design.

LINE

Line is beauty in itself. Line is the visual path the eye follows thus producing motion. The principle of line is one of the most important in any design. This essential has inherent qualities that appeal to our reason and senses. It may be severe and masculine, exhibiting strength and vitality, or it may be whimsical and feminine, expressing gentleness and delicacy. Its use provides the skeletal pattern and satisfies esthetic taste. Line is produced by the use of linear materials (stems, branches, or line flowers) or it is developed by the placement of round, mass forms in sequence, creating a feeling of direction. The height and character of line depends to a great degree on the growing habits of the plant. This repetition of plant form adds elegance and style.

The development of line may give balance, create rhythm, convey swift motion, or reflect repose, reverence, or other emotional qualities. The mood or theme of a design may be expressed with line.

120

Motion is created in sculpture and other art forms primarily by this element.

Line is never static; it produces a vibrant quality implying movement, giving a feeling of growth and life to the design. To maintain this, line continuity must never be broken. A restless quality and nervous feeling will be imparted by a design if line confusion exists. Cross hatching of stems or misplacing them so that they do not emanate from their logical origin causes a nervous reaction, breaks the rhythm, and the design appears to fall apart. In Figure 3, the composition lacks unity because no line pattern is developed. The undetermined direction of lines here cause discontinuity. In Figure 2, correction of line divergence is made.

The understanding of line, and its emotional qualities, enables one to make a complementary selection of flowers, foliage, and container to express a desired idea or mental picture. Let the furnishing of a room and the location of the arrangement govern line pattern of the design.

Today line "form," like our change in design concepts, assumes new meaning of great importance.

Line in floral design is thought of in a tridimensional manner. Drawing board representation on paper is the symbol; its suggestion, when translated from paper or mental image, becomes form. Periods in history are identified by line characteristics. As mentioned before,

Hogarth's delineation expresses rococo feminine charm, a time of delicate beauty. Today, the powerful, almost primitive parabolic arc is the most expressive. This line appears to defy the force gravity as in Plate 70. Its dynamic flow, may start with a long, forceful curve that seems almost straight, and end with an abrupt tense arc that appears to enclose space. The parabolic curve is a line of force, grace, and rhythmical balance; free of embellishment and irrelevant material, with a dramatic quality of simplified beauty, expressing spiritual thrill and satisfaction. The rhythmic body lines of dolphin fish and of airplanes show tense, swift forward motion that cuts through space, similar to the trajectory of a missile.

In this writing the author expresses his concept of contemporary "Line of Beauty" derived from the parabola, Plate 70. This example shows the directrix (a palm spathe) as a long extended sweep upward ending in a parabolic arc which returns the eye into the container. Each element in this design repeats the original curves acutely or in well defined forceful arcs. The curves developed in Entity, Frontispiece; Symphonic Browns, Plate 2; Arrested Motion, Plate 64, show virile force, strength and energy.

Plate 55, *Motion in Space,* shows visual motion carved in space by dynamic flow of line in this piece of ceramic art. The candle seems to be held in space by the ascending force of the swirling lines. It is representative of the current space age. The culmination of the design in the tall taper symbolizes today's thinking; the release from the earth's surface by scientific exploration. There was a time when man was held to the surface of earth; travel was limited to the horse; railroads were next; then the automobile and airplane followed. Now, scientists have released our thinking into space by launching the satellites free of earth's gravitational force. This is exemplified in this dynamic design of ceramic ribbons, creating its own pattern in space. Even the flowers appear to be released from gravity by being tangent to the swirling ceramic art.

Vertical Line implies strength, dignity, and severity, or may create formality of feeling. This quality is established generally by the firm placement of the main blossom. The arrangement is like an exclamation point. It demands attention!

In Plate 56, *An Etruscan Chalice* (476 B. C.), is an appropriate container for a vertical line arrangement. The first stem of aspidistra sets the linear pattern and all other materials conform to its placement, giving direction and force. It simulates the characteristic growth of the plant. The rhythm created in the variegation of the foliage accentuates the linear pattern. The addition of chartreuse Fuji chrysanthemums adds a color note in the monochromatic scheme, and their tiered positions give force to the design.

The rhythmic flow of undulating line in Plate 57, *Vertical Sansevieria,* originates at the margin of the free form, off white container, with cocoa brown lining. This graceful line flows into the bells-of-Ireland which blend themselves into the curves of the vertical sansevieria foliage. Cypripedium orchids, in rich mahogany reds and browns with green edges, repeat the color and shape of the container.

Vertical lines with gentle curves express serenity and dignity. The simplicity of the vertical arrangement in the modern glass hurricane globe in Plate 34, *Serenity,* illustrates these characteristics. An ethereal quality is obtained when the madonna or other religious figurine is used. The main lines of the arrangement are vertical. Even though the head of the figurine is bowed in humility, the line of thought soars upward and carries thought toward Heaven.

125

PLATE 57

Vertical Sansevierias

Rhythmic flow of undulating line originates at the margin of the free form, offwhite container with cocoa brown lining. This pulsation is immediately picked up by the vertical placement of sansevieria leaves entwined with bells-of-Ireland which blend themselves in spiraling motion.

Plate 20, *Aspiration*, illustrates the creation of line with various types of materials, expressing dignity and stateliness. The tall, linear snapdragons flow gracefully down to the line developed by the repetitious placement of the daffodils, thence through the tulips and terminating with the bunch of grapes. This picture illustrates the development of the Hogarth curve with a variety of flowers and fruit massed to create pattern. Each kind of material plays an important part, being grouped in its own line formation and blending with the preceding one. Plate 21, *"Line of Beauty,"* illustrates line by suggestion. Each variety is in a definite pattern of its own. The three stems of pussy willow of the upper section are repeated again in the

126

lower side of the composition, but appear to be continuous. The same effect is created by the bells-of-Ireland. Both are "tied" together with the "S" curve pattern of phalaenopsis orchids and pink roses. There are four Hogarth curves: one is superimposed upon the other, but each is complete in design. Strong distinction in the play of color and line patterns with various flower forms results from originality. Line in the entire design is one of simplicity, beauty, force, and movement. Space is carved by the segments of each division.

Borrowing from the Japanese symbols of heaven, man, and earth, Plate 58, *Contemporary Ikenobo*, callas rise in unison, creating a dynamic flow of line which portrays strength and growth. Repetition of the lines and blossoms in each segment of the design creates vibrant feeling and development. This design meets the demands of today — vision in motion.

PLATE 58

Contemporary Ikenobo

Borrowing from the Japanese symbols of heaven, man and earth, callas rise in unison creating dynamic flow of line portraying strength and growth. The wide expanse of water represents a lake. This design is vision in motion.

127

In Plate 59, *Tranquility*, the horizontal line is predominantly developed and is combined with the gently curved, vertical tree trunk. This cedar tree trunk is a symphony of continuous curves, beginning with the horizontal roll and slowly rising upward, then reversing itself. The spiral ginger foliage (Costus speciosus, called Crape or Malaya ginger) repeats the smooth twist of the cedar. The variegated agave leaf extends the horizontal line, ending in infinity. The gazelle's position reiterates the feeling of repose. Day lilies with their buds in tones of soft tan blend into the monochromatic color scheme; they are suggestive of fleeting moments. The whole composition is one of tranquility.

PLATE 59

Tranquility

The symphony of continuous curves in the cedar tree trunk begin with the horizontal roll and is continued by the agave leaf into infinity. This smooth flow of horizontal line with the resting gazelle produces a tranquil feeling. The fast fading daylily blossom is a transitory note of nature.

Horizontal Line when unbroken is more relaxing and informal. It implies repose and tranquility. When a straight or gently curved line is used in a horizontal position, it suggests the calm of a smooth sea meeting the horizon or the repose of an animal in the woodland. This line leads the eye along a graceful flowing path, giving the impression of quiet motion. It is more conducive to conversation than the restricted, vertical line and is useful for semi-formal occasions. The cornucopia container suggests this line pattern and exemplifies the bountiful harvest at Thanksgiving. Fruits and flowers flow horizontally over the board, developing the theme. Joy is expressed. A conch shell also suggests the horizontal line in the floral pattern, recalling the gently rolling sea.

Horizontal line when broken and jagged creates an entirely different quality, Plates 61, *Excitement,* and 90, *Study in Metamorphosis.* In Plate 61, *Excitement,* another emotion is produced by the broken horizontal lines. The gentle curves are replaced by sharp, jagged lines of the dominant driftwood serpent and tritoma. The directional poised position of the head and the opposite position of the tail creates force and feeling of attack. The tritomas contribute to this force by their piercing form and strong contrasting color. This flower arrangement shows a fascinating play of emotional quality created by line.

The low, formal, urn-shaped container used in Plate 92, *Formal Buffet,* lends itself to many floral patterns. Usually this container is associated with classical period arrangements. The horizontal line is developed with deep red Happiness roses and shell pink carnations. Velvety red cockscomb follows the diagonal line, tying the floral material together. Weight is added and a center of interest developed with the cockscomb. Caladium leaves outline the design. This arrangement is for a low, compact buffet or coffee table or a place on the mantel.

A curved line, whether vertical or horizontal, adds gentleness to an arrangement. Oriental appreciation of line quality is evident in American floral design. The old saying, "Curved is the line of beauty and straight is the line of duty," carries much weight in design development. Also, William Hogarth contributed one of the most important floral designs in his "Line of Beauty." In Plate 60, *Chinoiserie*, the Hogarth curve is developed by the sea plume and reiterated by the graceful, curving, bleached okra pods. The mass materials, teasel burrs, lotus seed pods, and artichoke blossoms, in sequence of size and repetition of placement add force to the curve. This is a play of line developed by the use of interesting materials (which were painted white and covered with mother-of-pearl). The Chinese pagoda, with the graceful figurine, is suggestive of the Oriental influence that invaded the Georgian period during Hogarth's day. This

PLATE 60

Chinoiserie

This arrangement shows the Chinese influence that invaded the Georgian period. The Oriental pagoda and graceful figurine form the focus for the floral pattern, a Hogarth curve. Delicate sea plume establish the line continued in the okra seed pods, then into the repetitious placement of round forms. All materials are painted white and covered with mother-of-pearl.

PLATE 61
Excitement

A broken ziz-zag horizontal line creates the emotion of excitement. Fascination and excitement in play of line is created in the horizontal direction force suggested by the materials. The poised driftwood serpent's head and tail create a feeling of attack which is reinforced by the form and strong contrasting red of the tritoma blossoms.

influence is found in furniture by Chippendale and in America at Williamsburg in the Chinese reception room of the Governor's Palace.

Lines In Accessories

When using a figurine or any accessory materials (driftwood, stone, etc.) to accent or complement the lines of a floral pattern, these materials must flow with the main lines of the pattern or complete those lines, carrying the eye back into the arrangement.

In Plate 26, *Oriental Grace*, the lines of the upper Scotch broom direct the eye toward the aged Chinese figure, whose shape is accented by the folds in his robe, and to the small child clinging to the man. The lower branch of Scotch broom with the table line carries the eye back into the arrangement. There is freedom of movement for the eye has secondary paths to follow. The up curved ends of this 250 year old Oriental Buddhist prayer table suggest by their lines the "frame" in which the eye is held.

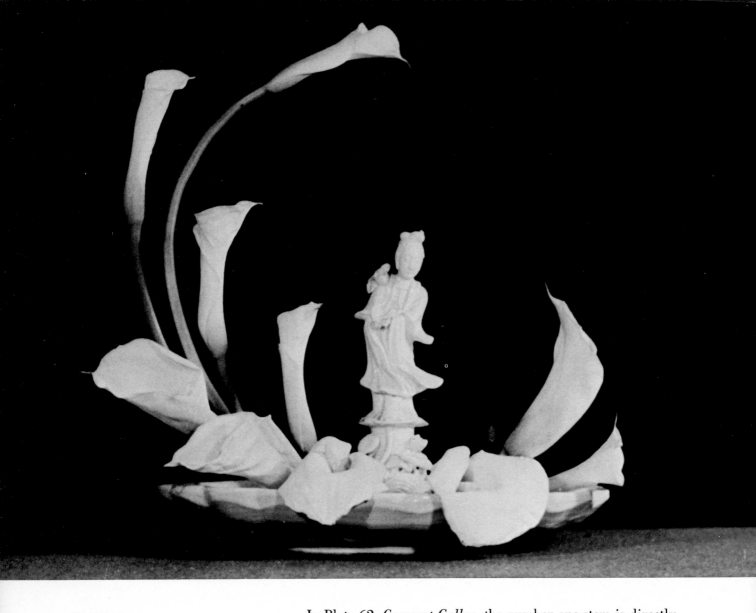

PLATE 62

Crescent Callas

The figurine blends perfectly in line with the circular motion of the calla blossoms.

In Plate 62, *Crescent Callas,* the number one stem is directly over the center; number two completes the design and the line of motion in the semi-circular design. The lines of the figurine flow with the lines created by the placement of the first two blossoms. The whole arrangement is a symphony of line and motion. Plate 63, *Flowing "S",* is similar to Plate 62, however, the number two blossom is reversed, creating a flowing S-curve which opens the design and carries the eye out of the picture. The lines of the figurine flow with lines of the main blossom. Had the figurine been used outside the arrangement to the right, its lines then would be reversed and flow back into the design. It would be necessary to select another figurine. (See Fig. 8)

132

PLATE 63
Flowing "S"

Flow of line has been diverted from the crescent design by the placement of No. 2 stem reversing the direction. This diversion opens the design and carries the eye to another location.

Fig. 8
Lines of a figurine must complement the lines of an arrangement.

133

In Plate 64, *Arrested Motion,* the directional force of line is strongly suggested. The ceramic pitcher creates the flow of motion which is repeated in the placement of the strelitzia. The container establishes the flow of line by its function. Strelitzia (bird-of-paradise) reinforces the direction of the colt's position and returns the eye back into composition. The curve of the handle is reproduced in the curve of the one leaf, then repeated in the curve of the legs and tail of the colt. The curves are to the outer edges of the design, while the points of the flowers and ears of the horse are to the inside. Dignity and strength are expressed in this composition. Flowing materials would be incongruous. This strength is reinforced by the selection of material. The startled stance of the horse expresses alertness and arrested motion.

Lines In Containers

When a line pattern is preferred, select a container to establish this design and complement its lines with compatible flowers. A container with straight or curved lines requires plant materials to accentuate its lines. By this selection the reward will be satisfying, that of creating a harmonious line-picture. To soften the lines of a design or add a touch of gracefulness, those plant materials which have natural curves should be used.

Containers with delicate lines need arrangements of delicate materials as in Plate 18, *The Three Graces.* Here the flowing lines in both figurine and sea shells immediately suggest the soft, flowing lines of the plant materials. One can feel the motion of the gentle, rolling sea created in this arrangement. Delicate curving line is vital in such an arrangement. The Scotch broom (painted white and covered with mother-of-pearl), repeating this rhythm completes the design. Strong, straight, rough textured materials arranged in dainty containers dominate, causing an arrangement to lack line harmony.

134

Again referring to Plate 42, *Danish Modern Hen,* the design value lies in the compositional lines of the original ceramic bird which gives character to this container. Birds-of-paradise (Strelitzia reginae) are used for they alone repeat in unison the lines forming the body of this artwork, and suggest in abstract the position of the head. Complete harmony in unison of line and color is achieved. The lines of this design are suggested and controlled by the container. The selection of materials is so sympathetic with the design that the floral element is one with the container.

Most contemporary homes have broad expanses of textured surfaces that are excellent for displaying accessories or flower arrangements. Such backgrounds are perfect foils for displaying arrangements of strong line. Flowers that are bold in line, color, and texture are striking when arranged in a container that exemplifies their qualities and placed in a room of modern decor.

The Early American home, or one of French influence, will tend to lessen the line value of materials. The traditional home does not often require a striking, contemporary design that dominates. An arrangement for such homes should blend with its settings and add a note of accent. The design in Plate 42 demands a background of textured expanse and would lose its value in a traditional home of flowered wall paper; whereas, the asymmetrical arrangement of Fuji chrysanthemums or similar flowers, Plate 25, would be perfectly at home.

The feeling of strength of an arrangement in a room can be increased by placing it so that it is not confined by space limitations or confused by nearby objects which detract from it. Avoid "busy" background patterns.

By studying materials closely, floral patterns are often suggested by their forms. Lines here become a vital element. The silhouette is of great importance and a valuable point to consider. It often gains as much value as line for accenting the skeletal pattern. Heretofore, in traditional design, the line in a flower arrangement was limited to the confines of the chosen geometric pattern. It was restricted to the circle or its segment, triangle, curve, etc. In *Free Form — Interpretive Design* line is not restricted. Only the principles of good design dictate the limitation.

RHYTHM

Rhythm is the apparent flow of line from the visual center of gravity or focal point, the repetition of materials giving force and movement without monotony, the sequence of color harmony and the gradation of the material size. Rhythm in music is the flow of melody. Rhythm in floral design is similar and imparts life and movement; it is the unity and flow of materials creating a pleasing eye image. It is accomplished by coherent use of the principles and elements of good design. Rhythm is achieved if the eye first sees the center of interest and then travels smoothly outward to the secondary features as in the traditional design, Plate 39, *Parrot Tulips,* or through inter-related units as in Free Form design, Plate 1, *Grecian Horse.* Any lack of transition in the floral design will interrupt smooth visual flow from one point to the other. Proper transition of elements and materials gives esthetic value to arrangements, creating a quality of excellence.

Some modern music often sounds strange and discordant; its melody is hard to follow, but when we become familiar with the melody and the mood the composer is trying to produce, we appreciate it. When the now famous piano concerto of Tchaikovsky (Piano Concerto #1 in B Flat Minor) was first performed it was badly received. The reviews were disheartening to the composer. Criticism at the time was strong; yet today this composition is famous and well loved. Rhythm is the keynote. Jazz bands took the melody and made

136

it the most popular theme of our time — it became trite in its familiarity.

"Whether I write well or ill," Tchaikovsky said, "one thing is certain — I write from an irresistible impulse. I speak the language of music because I always have something to say." This is the true expression of an artist — he must express that inner emotion as seen in one artistic form or another.

Although modern design may be advanced for some people, it cannot help but be appreciated as one becomes familiar with new forms. So it is with a flower arrangement — new, daring combinations or exotic designs are startling, but with familiarity they take on a new interest.

Rhythm is obtained through line creating motion, through repetition of materials, and gradation of sizes, and uses of color. In creating rhythm, line is important and its careful use imparts vitality, life and movement. Rhythmic motion is achieved in a design by line producing the proper perspective; it must arrive at a logical determined location, as in the discussion on *Line*. The interrupted flow causes the design to fall apart — rhythm is broken. In Plate 57 the rhythm, produced by the strong, graceful lines of the sansevierias, spirals majestically upward into space. The bells-of-Ireland blend perfectly into the rhythmic curve of the sansevierias and all but lose their individuality by emphasizing the rhythmic quality of the floral pattern. The sturdy placement of cypripedium orchids tends to hold the rhythmic flow of line in control.

In Plate 65, *Jungle Rhythm*, the element of rhythm is developed to the fullest extent. Nubian heads set the keynote for the development of this composition. Towering above their heads is the repetitious placement of dried desert spoons, representative of the beat, beat, beat, beat of the tom-toms; they increase in fullness with the sequential rise and brilliant color of the anthurium. These brilliant red anthurium reiterate the musical notes of the tom-toms in their

repetition and color. Strelitzia foliage adds dynamic force by its strong placement and severe shape. It is representative of the spears by which the natives gain food and protect their homes. Birds-of-paradise add motion of flight from the center of interest. Lush growth of the jungle is exemplified by the broad leaf rubber plant (Ficus pandurata) and the bananas. The container is a bath-board used by the Central American natives as a general utility utensil in domestic work.

Flowers of definite form and brilliant color are used to add force to repetition. Monotony is not evidenced here for character is portrayed in the selection of materials. Distinction is gained through skillful handling of materials. The sequence of color harmony is gained by gradation, contrast of chroma, hues, and values that carry the eye easily through a design, and by the logical use of the principles of balance, dominance, and contrast. Color rhythm is important, for Americans are more "color conscious" than other peoples of the world.

TEXTURE

Texture is relative; it refers to physical surface qualities of plant materials (smoothness, glossiness, roughness, etc.) or the composition of the arrangement of leaves, twigs, or branches on main stems. Leaf and stem patterns of plants affect texture. Slender elm twigs have a lacy texture if compared to the stubby branches of sturdy oaks. Ferns have a more delicate texture than huckleberry or salal (lemon) foliage. Earthenware has a rather coarse, rough texture even though it may be smooth to the touch; fine china, however, is delicate. In clothing material the texture is determined by the type of weave and the thread. The texture in floral design is embodied in the qualities affecting the senses of sight and touch along with associational values.

PLATE 65
ungle Rhythm

The beat, beat, beat, beat of the om-toms sets in motion jungle hythm. Brilliant red anthurium ecall the musical notes and with he repetitious placement of des-rt spoons beat out this rhythm. The anthurium shape represents he shields which protect the na-ives and strelitzia foliage sug-ests the spears by which natives ain their food and protect their omes. The flight of the birds-of-aradise adds motion.

139

Zinnias and marigolds grow pleasingly in the garden with roses, sweet peas, and other flowers, but they do not combine well with their neighbors in flower arrangements. As mentioned in the chapter on Harmony, a rather rough texture is associated with zinnias and marigolds when actually it is the stem surface that is giving them this quality; their petals are fine; however, they are best placed in pottery containers. Sweet peas always appear to be of fine texture, whereas roses are versatile and will blend with the finest down through rather rough textures.

In *Design* the texture of each part of a composition must be so related that it blends pleasingly with its neighbor, or it may be in strong contrast, causing one part to complement the other. Often bold, strong contrasts in texture add interest as seen in the interesting combination of texture in the free form arrangement of Plate 68, *Matate*. The container, primitive in design and fashioned from lava rock, has a very strong, coarse texture, with which the cypripedium orchids are in strong contrast. The transitional materials, echeveria and bleached desert wood, blend the two extremes in texture as does the native Guatemalan figurine.

In Plate 69, *Magnolias,* the soft patina of age has given this Chinese incense burner a fine texture which complements the quality of the magnolia blossom. The glossy foliage blends beautifully and is a transition between the flower and the urn. The same container is used in Plate 66, *Incense Burner.* Desert wood is stained with shoe polish to obtain the exact color of the tritoma blossoms. Their individual florets repeat the texture of the urn embodied in the raised design.

Cypripedium orchids are perfectly at home on tweeds or silks, and will blend beautifully in rough textured pottery or in fine containers. The texture of some flowers is relative and will either contrast with coarse dress materials or blend with finer ones. In Plate 67, *A Study In Rose And Green,* is an interesting display of tex-

140

PLATE 66 *Incense Burner*   PLATE 67 *A Study in Rose and Green*

PLATE 66

Incense Burner

Desert wood stained with shoe polish repeats the color of the tritoma blossoms. The textures of the wood and flowers are in contrast with the container.

PLATE 67

A Study in Rose and Green

Transition of texture is seen from the smooth quality of ti foliage and the large petals of peonies, into the fine texture of the frilly center petals, then into Lycopodium.

141

PLATE 68 *Matate*

Magnolias PLATE 69

ture; the blending is shown in easy steps from the old-rose, pink and green variegated ti leaves (Cordyline terminalis) through the smooth outer petals of the pink peonies, then into the fine texture of frilly, center petals, and this texture is repeated again in the lycopodium (L. cernuum — ground pine). This is an example of easy transition in flower form and accent foliage.

Texture also varies with color. Delicate colors (tints and pastels) usually have a fine textural appearance, e.g., light pink may appear soft and smooth. Brown suggests a rough texture and usually has a tweedy appearance and is associated with the Fall season and leaves rustling on the ground. It is also interesting to note that lavender is associated with feminine colors and, therefore, is of fine texture. This color is seldom seen in men's apparel; nor is lavender through purplish tones used in interior decor of general business offices. Spring colors are of delicate tints and expressive of infancy. Autumn colors are considered rather coarse and tweedy; they are stronger and more masculine.

PLATE 68
Matate

Strong contrast in texture is shown in the combination of the primitive lava rock container and smooth cypripedium orchids. The two extremes are blended with transitory materials of bleached desert wood, echeveria and Guatemalan native figurine.

PLATE 69
Magnolias

Age has given this Chinese incense burner a soft patina of fine texture which is complemented by the quality of the magnolias.

142

Chapter IV. Design

Chapter IV

Design

INTRODUCTION

A new concept has evolved from the floral work of the past. Contemporary trends and pure form, using basic principles of art, are forging into prominence. Freedom of expression currently evolving in floral art is indicative of the contemporary changes in other art forms such as painting, sculpture, and architecture. This modern trend is toward less conformity to fashion and tradition, simplification of materials, of presentation, and the yielding to international influences. Art changes, along with scientific advances, are producing a totally new culture. In any transition, much that is extreme and bizarre always appears, but inevitably there emerges from the experimental stages excellent examples of stable new art forms. The beauty, freshness, and vigor of the designs portrayed in this book speak for themselves. They justify the freedom of expression.

Design assumes a new, clear meaning. True creative ability finds a new path for expression without being encumbered by rules and limitations. Designing techniques are compatible with present day thinking, interior decor, architecture, and education.

Architects and engineers in various countries are creating a revolution in building forms today which is influencing allied arts and especially floral art. Eduardo Torrojo y Miret of Spain,

PLATE 70
The Parabola

The parabolic form, architectural in design, is seen in this saffron colored container. A curved palm sheath (directrix) of rich mahogany color forms the vertical arc encasing the globular yellow chrysanthemums. These chrysanthemums are repetitious of the vase form. Honey locust seed pods, tangent to the container, reiterate the parabolic curves and appear to be suspended in mid-air creating a fascinating area of incurved motion.

144

Pier Luigi Nervi of Italy, Mexico's Felix Candela and LeCorbusier of France are developing this new concept of space inclosure. Rhythm and super-strength are created by the interlocking of the hyperbolic paraboloid construction.

The "shellmen," as they are sometimes called, are creating this new form of architecture. This trend is one of the greatest deviations from international style since the Gothic arch and buttress were developed. These men working with concrete have referred to the material as "floating stone." Strength is derived from the parabola curve, egg shaped, which nature formed. They are proving that the parabola is the strongest form of curve. These architects from widely separated areas are gaining fame by changing the skyline and landscape with their conoids, cylinders, and spheres in double and compounded hyperbolic paraboloids. Their provocative forms in space are highly functional, with economy of space and cost of construction.

Webster defines the *Parabola:* "A plane curve, the path of a moving point that remains equally distant from a fixed point (focus) and from a fixed straight line (directrix)." An interesting fact, too, is that the parabola is similar in shape to the ancient weapon used by the Australians — the boomerang. The parabola curve is for contemporary decor where the interior is bold and striking, while the Hogarth curve in floral art form is delicate, graceful, and somewhat feminine, and is excellent with traditional style. (Figure 9).

Plate 70, *The Parabola,* turns to architecture for this lesson in design. The ceramic artist, Chabaneix, of France, followed the examples of Torrojo, of Spain and Pier Luigi Nervi, of Italy, in designing this artistic vase from the parabola. This saffron colored container has similar curves in its formation that make it harmonious with American mode of living. Planes cut the opening, giving new delineation as it is turned. To develop the floral pattern suggesting the directrix creating the parabola, the tall palm spathe of rich mahogany color is used which directs dynamic force into the con-

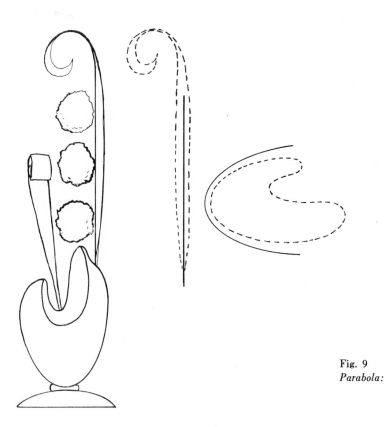

Fig. 9
Parabola:

tainer. This force is re-emphasized by the placement of globular yellow chrysanthemums in unison, creating rhythm through repetition, they are suggestive of the round form of the vase, and curves in the dried material and black, wooden base. Each unit appears to return into itself. The honey locust seed pods, tangent to and reiterating the main curves, appear to be suspended in mid-air, giving motion and accent to the parabolic curves. This container has value in design — it is a thing of beauty in itself. Floral material must accent its beauty and become a part of the whole to completely satisfy the composition.

The word *design* (pattern) is somewhat elusive and vague to many people who are starting in a new field of endeavor. They may see the "blueprint" on paper, but interpret the actual design with fresh materials they cannot. To clarify the terms in this book, design and pattern are used interchangeably; they are synonymous.

147

Each person has his own connotations of the word "design." Consider these definitions:

Webster:

Design — The arrangement of parts, details, form, color, etc., to produce a complete artistic unit.

Pattern — An arrangement of form, disposition of parts, or elements: design.

Other Authorities:

Design is a harmonious balance of all elements for a certain function.

Design is relatedness, togetherness in harmony.

Design is functional form.

Design is order.

Design is organization of materials in harmonious balance of all elements necessary for a composition.

Design is inter-relatedness, psychological effects of materials (associational value, shape, color, space, etc.).

Design must see the *Whole* (environs) as well as the *Focus* (single unit) — the things in full view at hand in relation to the final product.

Design (pattern) is the harmonious arrangement and balance of all principles and elements for the development of a single idea or theme. A design must not only have unity of composition within itself, but also be compatible with its setting to create a concordant whole; the environs, as well as the single unit, are seen — the inter-relatedness of the parts seen by the eye, plus what the subconscious mind sees. The psychological effects of materials — their associational value in addition to personal preference — influence our understanding of design. One will say an arrangement lacks design when actually it is his lack of appreciation, knowledge, or cultural background that is influencing his poor decision.

In the art of painting, Henri Matisse presented a "stranger" to his public, the picture, "Variation on a Still Life by DeHeem," 1915-17. This seemed bizarre at the time. The colors followed the Fauve school and the objects were painted in the Cubist manner of geometrical forms. Each item was more or less suggested, somewhat distorted and bold. Matisse stated, "What I am after, above all, is expression. . . ." Compare this work with the original by Jan Davids De Heem, "The Dessert," 1640 — it is traditional. The objects were painted as naturally as possible. DeHeem was intent on presenting the everyday materials as they appeared in life. The traditional painting appears warm and real for one can almost taste the fruit and feel the cloth. Matisse executed the same theme in his contemporary manner, but with impersonal feeling. Each object is for itself and the perspective vanishing point is indistinct. With DeHeem one sees the perspective immediately. Design becomes free with Matisse.

One holds to tradition because it is easy to comprehend; he is familiar with its design; there is no delving into the artist's meaning, for the full composition is immediately revealed. Unfamiliar work requires study. In contemporary design it is like meeting a group of strangers; at first they seem odd, hard to understand. The cultural backgrounds are different. One may dislike them intensely at first, but on becoming better acquainted, finding a common meeting ground which brings understanding, he grows to like these persons. *Free Form* designs are similar to the strangers, one begins to like that which he begins to understand. Some people never accept new friends or new art forms for they are not exposed to them frequently. They do not become educated to their value, whereas those who study, travel, and are aware of the trends and life about them accept and appreciate strangers and contemporary designs more readily.

In Plate 1, *Grecian Horse*, the use of Easter lilies in abstract form will startle some people because the lily is associated only with religious symbolism. It has perfect structural form, texture, and color for this arrangement. Here the lily is not used for its religious symbolism, or associational value, but for its pure abstract shape. Surely the Grecian Horse was never meant for a floral design in abstract, however, it is ideal for contemporary work.

To explain further how strongly tradition holds even a nation, in Oriental design a container is never used for anything else except the purpose for which it was made. In America there are no scruples in the use of any type container for decoration or floral design, regardless of its intent. It may be a Buddhist altar gong, (Plate 27), a vegetable dish, (Plate 93), or a piece of driftwood, (Plate 73), so far as it meets design requirements.

Until the introduction of *Free Form — Interpretive Design* floral patterns were derived from geometrical forms perfected by the Greeks in their development of architecture before the time of Christ. Grecian design principles were applied to all art — sculpture, painting, building design, etc. In America floral designers depended heavily on mathematical configurations established by the Greeks. The circle and its segments, the triangle, the rectangle, and conic sections were often employed as design vehicles. These geometrical floral patterns* are the principle contribution perfected by

Flowers: Their Creative Designs, by M. Benz

150

the great American Garden Club movement. They have their place and purpose today, however, creativeness is restricted if geometrical forms are to be followed exclusively. Limitations are thus imposed on the designers. Plant material has to be placed to conform to this pattern, rather than the material being appreciated for its own value. This value should be recognized and used advantageously. The intrinsic value of the flower, foliage, branch, or the wood-piece, is often lost when forced to conform to geometrical pattern. *Free Form — Interpretive Design* allows free use of materials. Configuration is governed only by the artistic ability of the designer and his interpretation of good art principles.

In painting there was one point of distance from which to enjoy the better view — where form, paint, effects of light and shadow, blended to form the perfect image. Geometric pattern was seen from a fixed perspective. Therefore, geometric design tended to become imitative. Many of the now "old masters" borrowed subjects, even to full compositions, from each other, but giving their own interpretations. For example: The theme of the painting by the great French artist, Edouard Manet, "Luncheon On The Grass," was inspired by Raphael's engraving of classical mythological river gods entitled, "The Judgment of Paris." Another example: Francisco Goya's "Majas on a Balcony," was again repeated by Manet in painting, "The Balcony." The compositions are similar, but in each case Manet gave the works a contemporary treatment. This was shocking at the time, because the public refused to accept the modern dress and starkness of delineation. The design seemed strange.

"Isms" developed due to the rebellion against realism:

IMPRESSIONISM appeared late in the 19th century (about 1870), reaching its peak in the 90's. Its adherents depicted quick visual impressions, giving a luminous quality by using broken colors, and the intermingling of touches of various hues. Read carefully the chapter on color: The effects of light and how the eye sees the complement of a color. The artists produced an atmospheric quality somewhat hazy in appearance, but giving the natural impression of the subject. Claude Monet was the greatest exponent of this form.

POSTIMPRESSIONISM returned to the old masters for design. They found that the most satisfying quality lay in the foundation or structure of the composition. Paul Cézanne, Vincent Van Gogh, and Paul Gauguin, are the most noted exponents of this form. Cézanne, one of the greatest among the group, rendered objects in the most practical way, using perspective, light, and shadow in an unconventional manner. He released painting from the one point perspective of traditional geometric design. He painted in abstract — freeing himself from the dictates of naturalism and the imitative demands of the public.

CUBISM originated in France about 1910. This form of painting was free of imitation. It reduced painting to design in space based on three dimensional geometry. The receding and advancing qualities of color were employed to show depth and to vary distances. Picasso is the most renowned artist of this group.

EXPRESSIONISM is the term used to describe art in which nature is subordinate to the expression of emotion. This is more spiritual in feeling. Instead of the extreme angular and distorted forms, Van Gogh employed graceful swirling curves that gave a fluid, rhythmic quality to his subject, e.g., "Road With Cypresses" (1889).

FAUVISM is the school of painting that deliberately distorts the object, using strong colors for emotional effects.

SURREALISM is suggestive of dreams and fanciful imagination, which resulted from Freud's psychological teachings.

In Plate 71, *Surrealism — Space Man*, a fanciful design is planned using a grotesque figurine that appears to have come from another planet. He has landed on the Earth, which is represented by the round cross-section of black walnut. The dark brown three-legged bowl holds other spheres, four yellow chrysanthemums, from which

PLATE 71

Surrealism — Space Man

A grotesque figurine appears to have come from another planet and landed on earth represented by the round cross section of black walnut. The dark brown three legged bowl holds other spheres, four yellow chrysanthemums, from which space man has arrived. Red cockscomb represents emotion encountered while he was on earth. Bleached twigs, in varied positions, show undetermined direction and turmoil of the human race.

152

Space-Man has arrived. The deep red cockscombs represent emotion encountered on Earth. Bleached twigs, Japanese paper bush, called metsumata (Edgeworthia papyrifera) in varied positions, show undetermined direction, and turmoil of the human race.

Free Form — Interpretive Design is pure design in the true sense of the word. It has independent personality that is appreciated for itself. It is timeless — it is not dated — as is shown in the works of art from the Grecian, Etruscan, and Roman periods that are used today in contemporary designs. Its intrinsic value is found in the esthetic beauty created. It evolves its own concept of design, but is based on the legacy of the past. A taste for elegance and luxury is shown through form, texture, and color, whereas in the past, decorative motifs were depended on to create "beauty." *Free Form* in design means unshackled imagination — guided by principles — free of tradition and man made rules. Floral materials speak for themselves in developing a mood, (Plate 59); a theme, (Plate 33); a travel experience, (Plate 98); or an accent note in interior design, (Plate 42).

In *Free Form — Interpretive Design,* all past geometrical figures or patterns that have restricted free creative ability must not be applied. Each viewer will find his own interpretation, Plate 30, *Entity* and Plate 76.

The timelessness of design is proved by the new discoveries of so-called primitive (ancient) art from the excavations in many countries, and from a study of museum pieces that are so priceless today. Plate 1 and Plate 56 are examples of pure art. The figures are as modern as though executed during this century. They blend with our living — the space age. The Greeks made art timeless through their sculpture and architecture. The Romans placed emphasis on grandeur, taking from their predecessors the best in art forms, making them their own. The Etruscans, in their art, showed a passion for motion and space, a life of gaiety and mysticism, and exaggerated the human figure, making it more expressive.

The statues recently discovered near Rome, Italy, sculptured by the Etruscans, circa 500 B.C., are considered modern in design by our standards. Their votive statues were never static but sculptured to give meaning, action in space, and form that resembled those of today. Plate 31, *Bali* — the figure is similar to the Etruscan votive figures.

Floral art today must express this timeless quality. *Free Form* is the expressive medium — the outlet for one's creative expression. The materials have always been available but one must appreciate them to see the possibilities that exist at our fingertips. It is today's mode of living, concept of distance, time, and space that affect today's floral design. A new vocabulary which describes the beauty and function of form must be understood to appreciate the intrinsic personality of floral art.

This new concept of floral design is influenced by space-form cutting its own design in atmosphere. Traveling was once held to earth's surface; the airplane released man. Then came travel by jet that released distance. Having passed supersonic speed, and then into space by missile — man appears ready to grasp the universe. Design was once held to earth's elements but we are now space conscious — e.g., design in the mobile. Heretofore, flower arrangements needed tables and containers, but today they are unlimited by space.

In Plate 72, *The Mobile,* the monkey is holding the long palm flower-panicle, to which is joined an interesting form of manzanita branch which becomes the "container" for the flowers. An orchid tube full of water is countersunk in this branch; the flower stem is run through a hole in the rubber cap which secures the stem in place. This mobile is suspended over a tropical pool in the author's home. Orchids, grown in his greenhouse as a hobby, are used in this manner. Air currents in the home cause the mobile to turn and goldfish in the pool create motion which adds interest.

In Plate 55, *Motion in Space,* the candle appears to be free of visible support. It seems suspended in space by motion, created by rhythmic flow of enveloping line. The ceramic piece further emphasizes this attribute by its defiance of gravity — its rhythmic ribbons of curves carving space to its own liking. Motion is the vital element created in space. In Plate 33, *An Allegorical Tale* — each elemental material appears to be free of the earth; a mystical quality exists.

Free Form — Interpretive Design, Contemporary, there are two groups: Realistic and non-realistic.

FIRST — *Realistic, interpretive,* follows the dictates of nature and tradition, though free of geometric pattern and rules of organization. This is most pleasing for one is accustomed to its design. The deviation from accepted form has not been too great. One feels at ease with this arrangement and readily understands the meaning of the theme. Like many contemporary works of art these designs are appreciated for what they are even though they do not blend into the individual's scheme of living. The arrangement has beauty and is appreciated not only for design of functional form and suitability of purpose with the decor, but for the intrinsic value of the materials. A beautiful curved branch or flower, either fresh or dried, is complete within itself or may be combined with the other features if desired. In Plate 1, the lilies may be omitted and the composition will remain perfect; or picture the statue of the horse removed and the design will be as pleasing as before with only the allium and container remaining. The sculptured dignity is inspiring. Here is pure abstract with linear form cutting into space, sculpturing its own form suggestive of the horse. The feeling is that of motion.

This is true with the rhythmic curve of the section of cedar tree in Plate 59, *Tranquility.* It is so satisfying that it alone is sufficient for design. The floral additions will enhance it, but are not necessary. One or more of the objects in the picture can be omitted and

PLATE 72
Mobile

Suspended from the monkey is the long palm flower pannicle to which is joined an interesting form of manzanita branch. An orchid tube full of water is countersunk in this branch to hold the flowers. The mobile is suspended over a tropical pool in the author's home.

157

not destroy the beauty. Again in Plate 73, *Driftwood Serpent*, flowers are an adjunct, not a necessity, to this pleasing piece of gnarled wood sculptured by nature. Floral materials are being appreciated today the same as cherished objects of art. The great architect, Frank Lloyd Wright, blended functional form and natural surroundings with such harmony that natural transition from one material to the other added emphasis to each. *Free Form* designing, likewise, considering intrinsic value, form, texture, and color, blends all units in harmony as one.

Simplification in presentation is one of the keynotes. In Plate 74, *Form*, strelitzia foliage, definite shape, is the object of importance. Its strong lines and spatula shaped leaves create pattern. They alone express beauty. The pairs of leaves, each in the opposite direction, placed in unison on the frog, originate as one stem (nemoto), creating rhythm in an unusual manner. The miniature pineapple adds strength to this rhythm by repeating the main line of the tallest stem and flowing into the osage orange (bois d'arc). The smooth surface of the black lacquered container and the leaves is in contrast with the rough texture of chartreuse fruit and russet pineapple. The crescent line of the fruit appears to be formed by the force of the descending foliage.

PLATE 74
Form

Spatula shaped leaves create design. The pairs of leaves originate as one stem (nemoto) producing an unusual rhythmic pattern. Dwarf pineapples and bois d'arc apples add a strong contrasting note of texture.

PLATE 73
Driftwood Serpent

This pleasing gnarled piece of wood sculptured by nature is appreciated for its parabolic form. It alone conjures fanciful illusions. Flowers are an adjunct, not to be considered a necessity.

PLATE 75

Abstract Birds

A non-realistic arrangement of flowers simulates Oriental calligraphy. Flame ginger blossoms race up the central stem like flames of passion. The cobra, coiled in defiance to man's regimentation, is poised to strike.

There is a structural quality that lends the design to open space allowing it to be viewed from any angle. As one learns in Oriental flower arranging, the design is placed in the tokonoma with flowers leaning toward the front. The faces of both foliage and flowers are presented and stems unite as one unit to form the nemoto. This is not true in most Occidental designs — the view is best seen not only from the foreground but from the sides; the back of the arrangement is generally toward the wall, except for table arrangements. *Free Form* arrangements are enjoyed from all angles. Plate 58, *Contemporary Ikenobo,* is a thing of beauty, a symphony of rhythmic

160

motion with a sculptured effect, and lines ascending into space. The floral patterns seen in Plate 6 and Plate 58 are identical. The author took advantage of the lessons learned from the classical Ikenobo school and accordingly used the arrangement for a centerpiece on a dining room table. *Free Form?* Yes; done to the designer's preference, reflecting international influence, but executed in a contemporary manner.

SECOND: *NonRealistic — NonObjective — Abstract* — The unusual use of materials producing form that is striking and bizarre with no illusion to reality. Abstract: To take from; materials removed from nature and used in a distorted form to emphasize a point.

Objects in this category are used to produce effect. Flowers give either color, texture, or form — not considering the blossoms in their natural state as such. True creative ability finds expression in emotion and inspiration. The term "abstract" is used in this writing to explain the use of materials in an unnatural manner but not to the point of distorted grotesqueness.

In Plate 75, *Abstract Birds,* the white birds-of-paradise (Strelitzia nicolai) are placed to show their full silhouette value and simulate Oriental calligraphy. Flame ginger blossoms race up the central stem like flames of passion. The cobra, coiled in defiance of regimentation by man, is poised to strike.

The formation of a new culture that is rapidly evolving produces this new concept of design. In contemporary work a structural purity is found, with a clear definition of form and bold frankness of expression. This freedom of design is made possible by the products of allied arts giving impetus to floral design, e.g., the ceramic hands in the frontispiece are examples which inspire the floral artist. This trend is found in architecture and interior decor.

In Plate 76, *Entity With Leaf,* a leaf (Monstera deliciosa) from the plant giving the blossom, has been added to the background reiterating the theme. The fingers of the leaf and those of the ceramic

PLATE 77
Motion in Space

The current space age is symbolized in this floral composition. Dynamic flow of motion cuts space to its own whim. The solid base is representative of the earth from which man has released missile into infinite space culminating in the tall taper.

piece complement each other and add rhythm to the all-encircling motion. The digits formed by the leaf and the fingers of the hand are one in abstract form. The uniform placement of the seeds on the spadix is representative of order — man's organization.

Only through careful study and knowledge of the materials, with thorough training in basic principles, logical planning, can we create a work of abstract art. In Plate 90, *Study In Metamorphosis,* abstract form is produced in the similarity of the segmented heliconia (H. humilis) florets and the strelitzia's boat-shaped bract. Color augments the personality of design though it is not a vital element, e.g., in black and white photography or stone sculpture. In Plate 77, *Motion in Space,* the fascinating ceramic piece used as a "container" is white, the tall taper and phalaenopsis orchids are of the same texture and color; the base is black onyx. Whether this design is seen in reality or in the black and white photograph, its intrinsic value establishes character. This design, like

PLATE 76
Entity With Leaf

A leaf from the plant giving the blossom has been added to the background. The fingers of the leaf and those of the hand are one in abstract form.

LATE 76

sculptured form, receives its value from graceful proportion, balance, and rhythmic flow of line. Color would not augment its value.

One's appreciation of these materials, i.e., his ability to recognize their value as to form and color as related to the whole picture, will allow him to create contemporary *Free Form* design, free of all man made rules and limitations, expressing his personality and individuality.

There are no formulae to follow or rules by which to judge — each flower arrangement has its own problems. Only the idea, the mental picture, being created is important. Study the shapes of the materials, the curves, the solid surfaces, their associational values — what do they say? — what do they suggest? — DESIGN.

GEOMETRICAL DESIGN

The construction of a flower arrangement according to geometrical patterns is similar to an engineering problem. An architect planning a home first decides on the general shape the structure will take. Ideas are sketched after studying materials and a proposed location. Plans are drawn to scale and little is left to chance. The floral designer, when planning to construct an attractive flower arrangement, can gain much by following the architect's example. It is not necessary to make a blueprint, but it is extremely important to have a picture in mind before starting to work.

The basic skeletal structure of a geometrical design can be established by the placement of the first three main lines. The development of the pattern is dependent on this foundation. In approximately 90% of the cases when an arrangement is "not right," the fault will be with the three stems establishing the form. Number one stem (or blossom) sets the height, number two stem gives the width in one direction and is generally horizontal; the number three stem sets the depth or the width in the opposite direction. It may be equal in length to the number two stem as in the formal triangle and oval pattern or shorter for the asymmetrical design. These three stems giving the height, width, shape or pattern, also establish the size of the arrangement. It is well to practice placing these stems in various containers to learn design and to get the feeling of balance and proportion, before completing the whole arrangement. Just as scales on a piano are played before learning to play a whole composition, practice is important.

In Oriental design the three segments (heaven, man and earth) are regulated as to their measurement and placement. However, the three stems forming the skeletal pattern in geometrical design, as introduced by the author in *Flowers: Their Creative Designs*, have no relationship to Oriental form.

Circular Patterns

The designs derived from a circle are the oval, round, fan-shaped, crescent, or segments of this figure.

Oval, Round

The full circular pattern is like a spot. It catches the eye and holds the viewer within the orbit. It leaves little to the imagination as compared to other geometrical patterns which lead the eye along graceful, flowing lines. The circular arrangement is excellent to use at the terminus of an axis, e.g., an altar in a church, or at the end of a room, etc. It has the quality of holding the viewer's attention to this location which makes it a dominant feature. Containers that lend themselves to this design are usually urn-shaped or similar types on pedestals.

In Plate 16, *Fifteenth Century Dutch*, the arrangement illustrates an oval mass design. Its pattern is established by the line flowers (snapdragons). A complete circular pattern is formed by the mass flowers and curved handle of this urn. To create interest

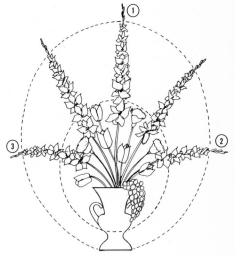

Fig. 10
Oval, Round.

165

PLATE 78
Easter Elegance

The oval pattern of white lark-spur is bisected with a graceful line of Easter lilies and rein-forced with caladium foliage within the design. Majestic daisies impart traditional texture.

within the oval pattern, an "S" curve is established starting with the upper left snapdraggon, flowing down through blue irises, white tulips, red roses, and into the grapes. A triangle of red roses is developed within the formation of the first three patterns; the oval, the circle and the "S" curve. This triangle of red roses adds strength to the design. To complete the circular pattern, the lower left snapdragon points into the tail of the bird accessory, the line curving through this bird continues through its beak into the face of a ranunculus blossom, and thus returns into the arrangement. Europeans are prone to arrange flowers in this manner. However, they do not place much emphasis on pattern when arranging flowers. Their gardens are small but bountiful; they collect a few blossoms from each plant and arrange them together.

In Plate 78, *Easter Elegance,* the oval pattern is developed with white larkspur arranged in a crystal Victorian lamp base. Easter lilies forming a diagonal line bisect the arrangement. Majestic daisies follow the line of the Easter lilies and are a transitional note

166

of texture between the larkspur and lilies. Emphasis is given the diagonal pattern by the use of caladium foliage within the oval. Feverfew to the left is given great importance by its position in the design and not scattered. The vertical axis is strongly evident, although bisected with the mass blossoms. This stately, exquisite design has enough importance to be dominantly featured.

Fan Shaped

In Plate 79, *Radiating Lines,* gladioli form the framework of the design. Each is equal in length and is placed on the frog to simulate a half-circle or fan. Red roses form a triangle as a center of interest and add color contrast. Line flowers as a rule develop this type pattern to the utmost; their lines suggest the radiating lines of the sun or the ribs of a fan. As in the oval and round, three main lines set the radiating pattern, and the remaining lines fall with the skeleton and are similar in length. Practically any round or oval design in a formal urn may be made into a fan by changing the container to a low type bowl as would be used on a mantel. The finished arrangement will be very similar. Ribs never alternate with two kinds of line flowers. Colors are never alternated, as a manufactured appearance is produced. Another pattern can be developed within this design and it is well to do so to avoid monotony. The element of motion is introduced by this second pattern for interest. One possessing a lovely fan may use it for a skeletal pattern and develop flowers at its base in line or mass to complete the arrangement. A similar pattern is produced by using a radiating palm leaf for background and a figurine or candle used with flowers to complete the focus.

Crescent Design

Portions of a circle are used effectively in floral design, forming a crescent or semi-circle. This pattern is most popular. It is compatible with a round mirror or tray background. Here the curved line becomes the vital element, motion is essential. The flowers may

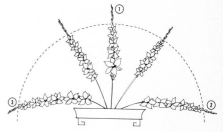

Fig. 11
Fan shaped, half circle.

Fig. 12
Crescent or portion of circle.

167

follow the crescent line or flow from it at a slight tangent but not perpendicular to it. An accessory may be added at the center, bisecting the design.

In Plate 80, *Sampan,* the black lacquered palm sheath with maroon lining, placed on an Oriental base, is reminiscent of small fishing vessels of the Orient. A gray dancing court figurine is the vertical axis. The lines of her body and those of the sampan suggest the lines of the floral pattern which is developed by red strap leaf caladiums and with accents of rich purple beauty-berries (Callicarpa americana). The tallest strap leaf caladium originates on the vertical axis of the arrangement. Its point and the hand of the figurine reinforce this axis.

In Plate 81, *Tropical Wind,* a fascinating semicircular design is created by the forceful foliage whose repetitious placement creates the feeling of winds that are so evident to the traveler. Form flowers, brilliant red flame ginger blossoms and miniature pineapple suggest the sturdiness of tropical growth which rebuffs the constant pressure of prevailing winds that shape natural growth in these areas.

If a figurine is used in a crescent design, the vertical axis running through the center of gravity should also pass through the center of the figurine. It is best used immediately under the No. 1 blossom. The lines of an accessory must repeat the curved lines of the semicircle (Plates 62 and 63). The figurine is not generally used outside

PLATE 81
Tropical Wind

The fascinating semi-circular design is created by the forceful foliage. Brilliant red flame ginger blossoms and miniature pineapple suggest the sturdiness of tropical growth which rebuffs the pressure of prevailing winds.

PLATE 80
Sampan

A black lacquered palm sheath on an Oriental base is reminiscent of small fishing vessels of the Orient. A gray dancing court figurine establishes the crescent floral pattern which is developed by red strap leaf caladium. Rich purple beauty berries complete the analogous color scheme.

169

the crescent for it does not complement. However, should this be desirable, its lines should complete the circular motion which is established by the number one stem.

The number one blossom is best placed directly over the center of gravity; the placement of the frog determines this point. No. 2 blossom will be shorter with the same curve and originating at the same point as No. 1, but flowing in the opposite direction, completing the circular feeling. No. 3 flower follows number one and additional flowers are placed accordingly. In Plate 62, the crescent figure is somewhat restricted and formal; however, it can be made less restricted by placing No. 2 blossom tangent to the curve, forming a flowing "S," (Plate 63). It is a pleasing design to the viewer. If a figurine is used within the design, its lines will flow with the curves of No. 1. If used to the outside, the lines of the accessory will flow toward the arrangement following the lines of No. 2 flower and carrying the eye back into the arrangement to complete circular motion set by No. 1. It is not advisable to select a straight lined figure for the outside position; it will conflict with the main pattern and compete for dominance and importance. (See figure 8.)

Plant materials used in arrangements of the semicircular pattern usually have bare stems and strong individual form characteristics. The stems have almost as much value as the flowers, because they contribute the element that is most valuable—line creating designs; callas, tulips, anthurium, etc., lend themselves beautifully. Carnations, when wired properly, may be used, since their leaf pattern allows this freedom. Other types (mass and filler) with composite leaf patterns and multiple stems may be used, however, their individual heads may be massed into the patterns, following each other in sequence.

In Plate 82, *Dance in Driftwood*, the heavy white fluted bowl supports the dynamic flow of line, circling the interesting desert wood which resembles the figure of a dancer in motion. This intriguing

170

PLATE 82

Dance in Driftwood

This intriguing piece of aged wood, showing evidence of erosion by wind driven sand, gives value to its imagery. Callas dance to the driftwood's vital rhythm.

PLATE 83

Sea Serpent

Undulating lines in the rich ironwood gnarl, picked up by the sprays of cymbidium orchids whose petals appear to create butterflies, form the crescent design in an ingenious manner.

piece of aged wood, which shows evidence of erosion by wind-driven sand, and is ornamented by chartreuse colored lichen, gives value to its imagery. The exquisite texture of the callas is in strong contrast to the bleached patina of the wood. The rhythmic position of callas adds swift decisive motion.

In Plate 83, *Sea Serpent*, the undulating lines in the deep red ironwood gnarl are picked up by the cymbidium orchids whose petals appear to create butterflies, forming the crescent design. The rich color of the serpentine gnarl is repeated in the lip of the green orchids. An unusual rhythmic pattern is created by the migratory flight of butterflies accenting the main lines.

171

Fig. 13
Hogarth Curve or Lazy "S"

Hogarth Curve — "Line of Beauty"

The adage "Curved is the line of beauty — straight is the line of duty," has more truth than poetry. No artist created greater beauty than did Hogarth with his curving lines. His name has been so associated with the double "S," that any curved line immediately has this connotation. This design is one of the most inspiring and demands attention. In garden club shows it has been a sure winner of first positions. Flowing grace, gentleness, softness, style, and fashion are but a few attributes of this type arrangement.

The development of the "S" pattern has many variations. Some designers prefer the line to be continuous and developed with the same blossoms; or it may be a suggested line developed with various floral materials, each repeating the line of the preceding one and flowing into the next; or the pattern may be one of suggestion where the floral material is seen at one end and reappears in the opposite direction.

In Plate 21, *"Line of Beauty,"* the roses form a continuous pattern which ties in three other similar patterns developed by suggestion. The phalaenopsis orchids, though separated by the roses, form a second "S" curve. Three bells-of-Ireland and three pussy willow stems appear above and below the roses and orchids, suggesting a continuous line through the design. When studying this plate, one notes that rhythm is created by a spiraling motion; it appears flat in the photograph, however the whole composition forms a convexed surface. The Hogarth "line of beauty" is developed by the tall, linear snapdragons flowing into the daffodils and continuing through the tulips, then into the grapes. The eye travels a natural, easy path guided by the sequential placement of the flowers.

In Plate 84, *Italian Bottle with Fruit*, the flowing "S" curve is first established by the dried, new growth of pine trees. The brown

172

color of the pine stems is repeated in the acorns which add force to the line. These flow into the larger fruits of the focal area which introduce lighter Fall colors. Bright red berries are interspersed through this area accenting the center of interest and adding a sparkling note of color to the rhythmic flow of line.

In Plate 85, *Harvest Alms Basket,* an unusual treatment is shown in the development of the "S" pattern, suggesting the garland and baskets of fruit representative of the Grecian and Roman periods. The seed stems from date palms establish the "S" curve pattern along with the triangular grouping of alms baskets. This pattern is reinforced with the dried okra seed pods and the graceful assembly of fruits and nuts. A golden artichoke blossom reversed, showing the stem end outward and with an agave seed cluster surrounded with red cherries, forms the center of interest.

173

Triangular Designs

The third geometrical figure is a triangle, which is either symmetrical (formal) or asymmetrical (informal) according to the degree of the angle. The patterns derived from this figure are very interesting and pleasing, and it is one of the leading designs of American flower arrangement. This design yields greater beauty with less flowers than any of the other geometrical forms. It stimulates the imagination and carries the eye through its various parts or to another object of importance.

The three segments working in opposition with one dominating is comparable to the Trinity in religion, mystery story plots, love stories, Oriental design, etc. So it is with proportion; there is the all important 1-3 relationship. One will dominate, so it is in the triangular design, the upright line dominates and controls placement in this form. The other lines are subordinate and are used to emphasize.

Triangular pattern may be used as a line, a mass or combination of line and mass arrangement. The most frequently used is that of line-mass.

SYMMETRICAL TRIANGLE

The symmetrical triangle is formal and man made. It is in perfect balance, having the elements of one side similar to those of the other and equally distributed about the central axis. The No. 1 blossom establishes the height of the arrangement (apex of the triangle) and is placed directly in the center of the container. The No. 2 and No. 3 blossoms are equal in length and extend out to either side establishing the width. They lie horizontally over the edge of the container, completing the other two points of the triangle. Additional material falls within the three points of the triangle. This additional material may form a graceful, sweeping curve within these boundaries, or it may adhere closely to the three main stems forming a severe, stylized

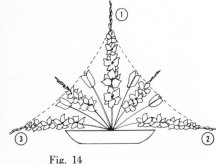

Fig. 14
Symmetrical triangle

contemporary design. Should flowers or foliage cross the lines connecting the points, it would tend to make the design approach a fan arrangement.

In Plate 86, *Georgian Epergne*, a note of elegance is expressed in the silk damask background and the exquisite container. The entire setting is one that expresses formality which immediately suggests the symmetrical triangle. Deep red happiness roses dominate the arrangement and are enhanced by the fine quality of the silk damask. Pink roses add a lighter color note. Lilies-of-the-valley and sweetheart roses with clusters of violets are flowers that were favorites during this period. Clusters of wine-colored grapes add to the lushness of this design. The side arms adding symmetry hold tussy-muzzies of sweetheart roses and violets.

Plate 87, *Formal Balance*, is an exquisite example of a Directoire compote with silver plateau arranged in formal balance with Spring flowers. This compote suggests formality which immediately

PLATE 86
Georgian Epergne

Elegance is expressed in the silk damask background and exquisite container. The entire setting expresses formality and is developed in the symmetrical triangle of deep red Happiness roses. Lighter pink roses, lilies-of-the-valley, violets, and grapes complete this design. The epergne's side arms hold tussy-muzzies of sweetheart roses and violets.

175

PLATE 87

Formal Balance

A Directoire compote with silver plateau holds an exquisite example of formal balance with spring flowers. The points of the symmetrical triangle are established with blue irises. Pink ranunculi, daffodils, and an "S" curve of rose pink tulips complete this design.

establishes the symmetrical triangular design. The points are established with blue irises whose lines descend into the arrangement and are immediately picked up with accent flowers of pink ranunculi and daffodils. A Hogarth curve is developed with rose-pink tulips which unite the stem of the compote and the central axis of the floral design. This graceful flowing line creates rhythm and relieves the stiffness of the formal pattern.

When combining several types of flower forms, one may use line flowers to establish the pattern outline (skeleton) and mass flowers within the framework as in Plate 88, *Symmetrical Triangle*. The apricot-colored gladioli (line flowers) establish the equilateral triangular pattern. Two gladioli are shortened and placed on either side of the vertical stem, No. 1 blossom. A curved line is created from the apex of No. 1 blossom down to both sides ending

176

with points of No. 2 and No. 3 blossoms. Daffodils are added on a cross-diagonal, complementing the line of tulips on the opposite side. The color at the base of each tulip petal is the same brilliant yellow of the daffodils.

On occasions when a long, low arrangement is needed as for the centerpiece for a dining room table, or a banquet table, the No. 1 blossom is held within 14 inches in height. The No. 2 and No. 3 blossoms are extended as far as the table will allow, considering the number of guests to be seated (see the chapter on proportion). For formal occasions, teas, buffets, etc., the arrangement may be as high as the proportions of the room will allow. In Plate 44, *Formal Tea,* the symmetrical triangle is developed. The floral pattern is similar, however, no line flowers are used. Blue irises establish the triangular design and it is developed with other Spring flowers.

PLATE 88
Symmetrical Triangle

Apricot colored gladioli form the equilateral triangle with daffodils on one-cross diagonal and tulips on the other, blended to render an interesting treatment.

177

SYMMETRICAL TRIANGLE — VERTICAL CONE DESIGN

The cone or conoid design is similar in shape to the pyramids, although round in form. To be dramatic, it must be tall. This pattern was first used in the Near Eastern culture especially during the Byzantine period. The Turkish turban is suggestive of this particular design. It may be developed by using foliage closely applied to a conical foundation with ornaments of clustered fruit or a garland of fruits and flowers spiraling from its base to the apex. In formal urns, this pattern may be developed beautifully, using solid masses of blossoms or foliage for design on a newel post, or a pair of arrangements to either side of a mantel; floral development in this manner is dramatic.

In Plate 14, *Baccarat Byzantine Cone*, the spiraling standard of the crystal epergne is suggestive of the Byzantine cone and Turkish minaret. The flowers are arranged in a contemporary manner developing a cone and it is belted with callas which contribute to the formality by their form.

In Plate 45, *Floral Fountain*, the tiered formation of the chrysanthemums is representative of the conoid. The teasel burr at the top is similar to the pineapple used extensively as a decorative motif in the Byzantine period. The tiered position of chrysanthemums being separated by a layer of split palm sheaths circling over teasel burrs creates stratification presenting an unusual composition. The repetitious placement of units gives formality of design.

In Plate 89, *Vertical Cone*, another dramatic effect is expressed. A crystal Victorian lamp base holds three yellow gladioli in graduated lengths, bringing the eye down into the repetitious

PLATE 89
Vertical Cone

Dignity is expressed by this vertical cone shaped arrangement of yellow gladioli and daffodils. Red carnations give mass and importance to the daffodils. To maintain the formality of the cone, three gladiolus leaves are used opposed to their blossoms.

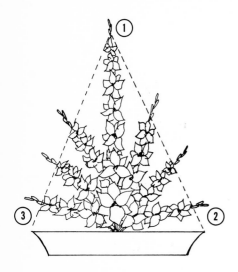

Fig. 15
Vertical triangle or cone.

placement of yellow daffodils. The gladioli form the upper portion of a cone which is completed with red carnations. They are used as background for the daffodils and add color contrasts. To maintain the formality of the cone, three gladiolus leaves are used on the opposite side, repeating the three tips of the gladioli. Dignity is expressed by vertical line.

In Plate 40, *Symbolic Numbers,* the vertical cone is developed with gladioli, and an "S" curve of tulips creates graceful flow of line in the formal design. The figurine is accented by the dark green ficus leaf with an outline similar to the cone.

ASYMMETRICAL TRIANGLE — VERTICAL RIGHT ANGLE

There are two important patterns in floral design derived from the asymmetrical triangle. The first is the right angle design whose tall main line is perpendicular to the base. The second one is called scalene; its central axis is at an oblique angle to the base thus causing unequal sides and angles.

The asymmetrical triangle is natural and pleasing; it lacks the restriction of perfect symmetry and is therefore informal and relaxing. Its asymmetry stimulates the imagination more than other geometrical patterns. It shows the vigor and vitality of plant growth. Note that there is good balance; many novice arrangers seem to confuse the meaning of asymmetrical design with off-balanced arrangements. In American homes free of definite foreign decor this design is preferred. Oriental flower arrangements follow this pattern only, for it simulates the natural growing plants. As mentioned in the history of flower arrangement the mode of Oriental living and entertaining does not require formality of design (equilateral triangle) as Occidentals understand the term. They do not have furniture which requires symmetrical designing.

The focal point generally is developed toward the high side of the arrangement in an oblong or rectangular container. When using a pin or cage frog, it is secured toward this high side, or when

180

using chicken wire for the foundation, the main stem will be secured to this frog toward the high side. The extra portion of container on the low side of the arrangement helps counterbalance height and gives good visual balance. A line drawn from the apex of the No. 1 blossom to the tip of No. 2 flower forms the hypotenuse of the triangle. This line must not be crossed with flowers or foliage. It is best to develop a sweeping curve uniting these two points. No. 3 flower of the skeleton may be placed between the first two dividing this space equally; or it may take the position to the outside of No. 1 and is shorter than No. 2 blossom. Thus the three stems form the triangle.

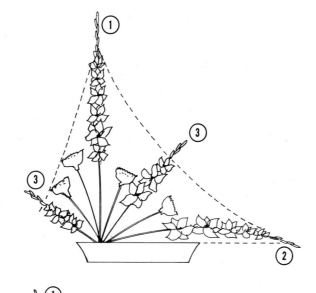

Fig. 16
Asymmetrical triangle, right angle.

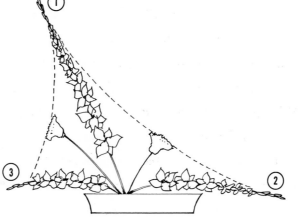

Fig. 17
Asymmetrical triangle—Scalene.

181

In Plate 47, *Fuji and Caladiums*, the bowl, which is spherical, more or less demands that the central stem No. 1 be placed in the center and not to the off side as discussed above. To maintain equilibrium the flowers and foliage have been carefully distributed to either side of the central axis thereby obtaining weight and visual balance. The use of the caladium leaf in full view on the right hand side adds importance to the No. 2 position. On the left of the arrangement a Fuji chrysanthemum terminates position No. 3. The caladium leaf to the rear is shorter than the No. 3 blossom and therefore not competing in importance.

In Plate 38, *The Pulque Jug*, perfect rhythm is created in the asymmetrical design. The desert driftwood placed to the left of center dominates the composition. It suggests the three blossoms placed one above the other forming the main stem (No. 1). They repeat the three segments of the driftwood and flow forcefully down into the two "birds" on the right forming No. 2 point of the triangle. To the left, two "birds" are used for position No. 3 and are carefully placed to pick up the line of the third flower of the main stem. The termini of the lines converge at the base of the Guatemalan figurine and are tied in one position with agave plant. This plant's radiating leaves add force.

Generally the asymmetrical arrangement is made with a high left and low right unless otherwise influenced by its placement. Since Americans generally are accustomed to the left-to-right motion, the design appears more natural (this is discussed fully in Chapter 3, Principles of Design, under the topic of Balance). This left-to-right motion will vary when the environs of the room dictate differently as in Plate 48, where the staircase cuts the wall surface forming a triangle. The floral pattern must conform to this restriction. The upper stock blossom is a continuation of the container and indicates the vertical terminus line of the staircase, forming the right side of the design compatible to its setting. The lower left stock blossom completes the triangle and carries the eye to the vase and candlesticks. The position of the horse continues the dominating descending line of the staircase. A careful grouping of fruit to the right hand counterbalances the arrangement in weight and color. (See chapter on Asymmetrical Balance.)

ASYMMETRICAL TRIANGLE — SCALENE

Scalene triangles are the second type of asymmetrical design. In geometry the word denotes a triangular figure with unequal sides and angles. The axis is not perpendicular to the base but on the oblique beginning with the high side terminating at the frog but indicating the direction of the lower side. This pattern gives the impression of a greater quantity of flowers. Its pleasing, sweeping motion is apparent due to the absence of stiff right angles in the lines forming the skeleton.

The No. 1 blossom is placed off center to the high side and leaning backwards. Depth is gained in this placement. No. 2 stem is shorter and more fully developed thus giving weight. It is placed a little forward over the edge of the container in a horizontal position, uniting the container with the arrangement. One common fault of the beginner is having this second stem too upright which causes an awkward effect. The No. 3 blossom is either between the first two or placed to the opposite side of the main stem from No. 2. It is never placed near the second stem because the structural pattern would be lost.

In Plate 37, *Harmony*, the scalene triangle is developed with eremurus lilies and completed with the grouping of fruit and flowers in the weighing pan to the opposite side of the scales. Although the weighing scales suggest the formal balance, the development of the floral pattern has been completed in a scalene triangle.

Horizontal Arrangements

Horizontal arrangements are interesting although infrequently used. The lines suggest repose and tranquility when unbroken. However a broken zig-zag horizontal line creates excitement and unrest which implies swift motion. It requires careful handling to overcome the informality thus created. Plant characteristics generally place certain requirements on the arranger, that of portraying natural habits of growth to best advantage. These restrictions must be artistically mastered in design to use vertical growth in a logical horizontal manner. Free use of material is a person's prerogative but logic demands its rights. In Plate 59, *Tranquility*, the horizontal feeling is predominant even though vertical line has been incorporated. In Plate 61, *Excitement*, the horizontal line has been severely interrupted by the striking pose of the serpent and the jagged line of the tritoma, whose brilliant, fiery color adds to the emotional response. These two illustrations are diametrically opposed in feeling but illustrate line pattern in horizontal design. The plant materials in these illustrations are in a natural position. A third illustration of horizontal design, but using plant material in an unnatural position (abstract) is shown in Plate 90, *Study In Metamorphosis*. The heliconia (H. humilis) generally droops from stiff upright stalks; however, it is used to continue the horizontal line of the yucca bloom stalk cut on a bias. The heliconia florets create the zig-zag jagged line of excitement. The sheath of these flowers defines a severe horizontal line across the yucca container. The bracts of strelitzia repeat the bracts of heliconia floret, marching across the container with rhythmic repetition.

The container will more or less regulate the development of a horizontal arrangement. A cornucopia used for a Thanksgiving table is an excellent example. This container suggests a bountiful harvest overflowing on the board. Fruit and flowers will follow the

PLATE 90

Dynamic Metamorphosis

A non-realistic use of plant material is shown in horizontal abstract form. Heliconia, which generally droops from stiff upright stalks, is used for its jagged sawtooth effect to produce excitement. The swift impatient line is continued with bracts of strelitzia. The base, a yucca stalk cut on the bias, adds force.

185

line of this container in a smooth easy manner. Sequence of size from the mouth of the container terminating in a small fruit or line material repeating the point of the cornucopia is needed. Conch shells also lend themselves to this design as do low bowls whose sides flow outward. Table baskets made of silver, crystal, or dresden, are exquisite when designed with a horizontal pattern.

In Plate 91, *Spring Flowers,* the container is a combination of two vertical cornucopias, whose lines suggest the horizontal pattern. Informality is introduced by the use of candy-tuft, flowing to either side with purple anemones giving mass and color.

PLATE 91
Spring Flowers

The container is a combination of two vertical cornucopias whose lines suggest the formal horizontal pattern. Informality is introduced by the use of graceful candytuft flowers to either side with purple anemones adding mass and color.

186

PLATE 92
Formal Buffet

The formal shaped container of classical influence lends itself to a horizontal arrangement. Alternating rows of deep red Happiness roses, pink carnations, and velvet cockscomb on the cross diagonal are combined in this arrangement designed for formal buffet or coffee table.

In Plate 92, *Formal Buffet,* the footed formal urn is given an unusual treatment. Generally this urn, showing classic design, is thought of as either a round or triangular pattern. The flow of line in this urn is on a diagonal developed with deep red roses alternating with pink carnations. This grouping is held in position by red velvet cockscomb whose dark color and weight are sufficient to give good visual and color balance. This pattern is accentuated by caladium foliage repeating the pink and red colors; its solid surfaces supply needed weight to the design and its points verify direction. A light fern-like foliage would be too delicate even though it blends in texture; a mass effect is needed.

187

Rectangular or Square Arrangements

Rectangular or square arrangements are not often used because the element of dominance is usually lacking. One corner competes with the other and the mind is confused. Equals cause conflict — unrest. To eliminate this hazard a suitable background or picture frame will aid greatly. This background must be an integral part of the design, thus through the power of suggestion this conflict will be eliminated. Voids have almost as much value as the flowers; they give relief from competition and allow the flowers to dominate. In Plate 93, *A Morn-*

188

ing Surprise, the square background with the rectangular vegetable bowl is used to establish the flower arrangement pattern. Daffodils are arranged in a naturalistic manner, showing the influence of Oriental Moribana style. Note how the void carries almost as much interest and weight as the flowers. The harmony of container, background, color, texture, and flowers is so blended that the mood and theme become one. Simplicity is the keynote. Unity in this illustration shows how the smaller right hand grouping of flowers aided by the open space of the background has almost equal importance with its neighbor to the left.

DESIGN POINTS TO REMEMBER

1. Have a mental picture of the design before trying to arrange — this will save hours of time and damage to the flowers.

2. In poor designing, when it just does not "look right" — the fault is generally with the placement of one of the first three stems — the skeleton or foundation.

3. Crowding detracts; let each flower retain its individuality except in abstract design. In abstract the flowers may be used for color, texture, or form.

4. Multiple centers of interest are confusing. There should be only one and it should be where the lines converge. Do not have a "bull's eye" development at this point. *Free Form* design need not have the well defined center of interest that is desirable in geometric patterns. Read carefully the chapter on *Free Form.*

5. In geometrical design the container either blends or is subordinate to the arrangement. In *Free Form* the container may be the featured point of interest and flowers only an enhancement.

6. Geometrical Design: the top margin of the container is broken with foliage or flowers flowing over the edge to add unity.

Free Form: The margin of receptacle may be fully free. The lines of the foliage and container so complement each other that there is unity. Plates 2, 6, 36.

189

7. Attain balance without perfect symmetry, thus preventing rigid formality. Naturalness is the result.

8. Strong lines, or heavy color, or open blossoms used low give stability and balance.

9. Geometrical Design: an uneven number when less than eight is generally easier for the beginner to arrange. This prevents a manufactured look of sets of 2's and 3's.

Free Form: one is concerned with design only, not numbers.

10. Alternating flowers or colors will give a "sandwich" appearance.

11. Absurd combinations become garish — conflict. Contrast is good, though it must be logical.

12. Take advantage of the natural curves and lines in flowers and foliage. Distinction is gained. This adds grace and beauty; creativeness is expressed.

13. Keep form flowers prominent. Generally only one of this type is to be used in an arrangement. Do not crowd them.

14. Eliminate foliage that rots under water.

15. Arrangements for round tables should have three points horizontally. Two will bisect, dividing the table in half. Four points will form an X which is poor in design.

16. When using a few flowers in a design, group them smartly in a definite structural pattern.

17. Do not use a clear, transparent container for a design when using stems that become slimy in water.

18. While arranging flowers step back to get the proper perspective, viewing it from the angle that it will be approached.

19. *Free Form* design is seen from all angles.

20. Flower arrangements for exhibition purposes or competition in flower shows must comply with the rules of the organization, even though a person is restricted in his creative ability.

190

Chapter V. Color

Chapter V

Color

INTRODUCTION

Aside from personal preferences, the *Language of Color* is universal. Color has the same psychological effect on the natives of the Yangtze Valley as on the natives of Kankakee, Illinois. Color strongly influences emotion. One color creates an atmosphere of warmth, another produces a cooling quality; others may add dignity or informality.

The psychological effect of color is generally the same for all people; however, preference, impact, and meaning vary with individuals. People react differently to the same color, but generally speaking a person's reaction to color is influenced first by his nervous response and secondly by his educational training (environment). Considering the first: Color is seen as the result of a stimulus (light) reacting on the retina of the eye. This response is transmitted to the brain which registers the stimulus — thus color is seen. Each individual will naturally react according to his personality. This personal response gives individuality and originality to a design. The second cause of color preference is influenced by his native homeland which is affected by the intensity of the sun. His homeland governs his youthful training and education. The term "education" in this instance implies childhood training, and the regional color preferences of the area during his formative years in addition to his schooling. Education is knowledge gained from everyday associations with his fellow man; experience. A person from the tropics often has a liking for brilliant colors, a taste for highly spiced foods, and he usually possesses a strong personality and quick temper. Nature repeats this brilliancy in the plumage of the birds, vibrant colors of flowers, and the luxuriant plant growth. People coming from the cooler climates where the sun is less intense prefer subdued colors. They have to be educated to the appreciation of intense, rich color and spicy foods.

Color hues have developed symbolic meanings in various countries, and tradition and symbolism are reflected in color connotations (flags, emblems). White stands for purity in the United States, while in China it means mourning. Here black is the mourning color. The native Indians of Guatemala use the petals of orange flowers when praying for the Souls in purgatory and white petals for the Souls in Heaven.

Historical periods had color schemes. The Victorian era used jewel tones, rich reds and purples with trims of gold. American provincials used warm gay colors. The contemporary trend is toward contrasts of almost pure hue.

An understanding of the function of color and a mastery of its use increase the versatility of any person and strengthen the ability to create desired atmospheres and effects. Through use of almost any color, desired impressions can be easily produced.

To illustrate this, consider the merrily chatting dinner guests who walked into a Chicago hotel's dining room and took their places at the table. As they did, the lighting underwent a subtle change. Within a few minutes some of the guests were violently ill, others mildly sick, and all were without appetite for the exceptionally fine food that had been prepared for them.

The celery on the table had turned a gaudy pink, the steaks a whitish grey, the tall glasses of milk were a blood red, and the salads a sickly blue. What had been fresh green peas one moment were black over-sized caviar the next. The side dishes of peanuts were a weird crimson.

It was not a demonstration of magic, but an interesting experiment to determine the influence of light and color on human senses. Instead of the usual dining room lights, the host had illuminated the room by especially designed filter lamps which cut out all colors of the spectrum except green and red. The host, a lighting engineer, thought his guests would have their stomachs turned — his experiment was a success. After restoring normal lighting he told them that it was a demonstration of the effect of light and color; not only on the sense of sight but upon the related senses of taste, touch, and smell. Color, he reminded his guests, could excite and stimulate a person acutely.

The result of this color experiment demonstrates the value of color as a potential tool to trigger human reactions and desires. Often color dislikes are caused by association with an early childhood experience. Blonds who were forced to wear blue during their childhood usually have a dislike for the color. Few people realize the great psychological impact of color on our health and happiness.

Color gives life and personality to designs. Harmonious colors produce designs that satisfy even though they lack structural quality. Conversely, if arrangements are perfect in form, but poor in color selection, the results may be unpleasant. Design can exist without color and be esthetically beautiful, but color in flower arrangements cannot be art without design.

Color is just as important to a work of art as its structural pattern (design) or shape. Design (the skeletal pattern of a piece of art) pleases the sense of physical balance and proportion, while color satisfies the esthetic taste — senses of sight, taste, touch, and smell. As illustrated in photography, a black and white picture shows the skeletal pattern only, stripped of the influence of color. The beauty lies in the relationship of its parts which takes into account only balance and proportion. The addition of color to these photographs will cause excitement. This quality is stimulated by the addition of the enormous influence of color. A composition out of balance and proportion, but striking in color combination will be satisfying, however the same arrangement in black and white will reveal the poor design. It is the color combination that makes the composition beautiful.

It is not necessary to understand color theory or the scientific facts concerning color to make beautiful floral arrangements, just as it is not necessary to understand the theory of the internal combustion engine to drive a car. It is imperative, however, to know and understand human reaction to color and how to skillfully employ it.

COLOR CHART AND SPECTRUM

The center colors (red, yellow, and blue) are the primary colors from which all others are made. They are the building blocks for the entire color pigment system. Nature has provided red which is advancing, exciting, and warm; blue (directly opposite to red) is receding, cool, and quieting; yellow is brilliant and cheerful. An advancing red, a receding blue, and a brilliant yellow to brighten are the primary color tools.

The mixture of any two primary colors produces a secondary color: orange, green, or violet:

orange — yellow and red

green — blue and yellow

violet — red and blue

The proportion of the primary color in a mixture is important. In orange, if there is a greater amount of yellow than red, yellow-orange is produced. If a greater amount of red is used, the result will be a red-orange. The same is true with other color mixtures. More yellow in green makes a yellow-green, and more blue makes a blue-green; more red in violet makes a red-violet, and more blue

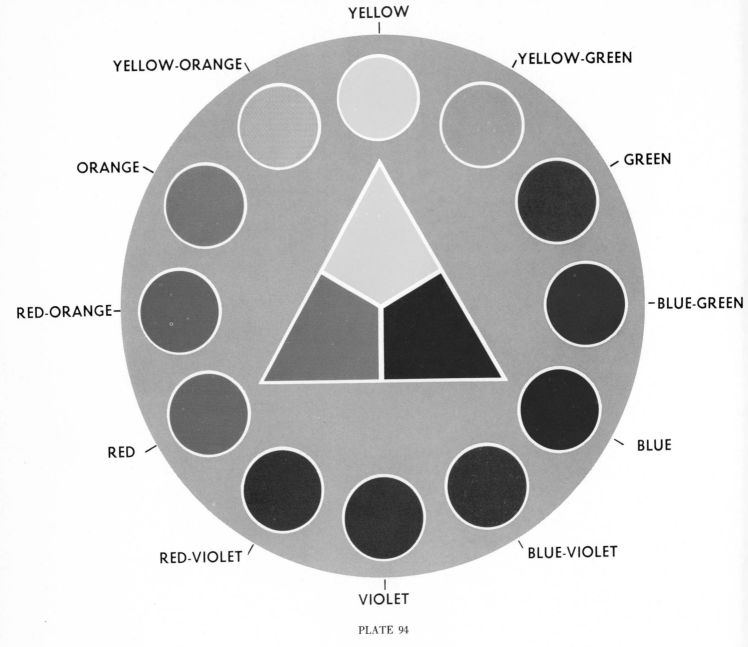

YELLOW

YELLOW-ORANGE

YELLOW-GREEN

ORANGE

GREEN

RED-ORANGE

BLUE-GREEN

RED

BLUE

RED-VIOLET

BLUE-VIOLET

VIOLET

PLATE 94

COLOR CHART

PLATE 95

SPECTRUM

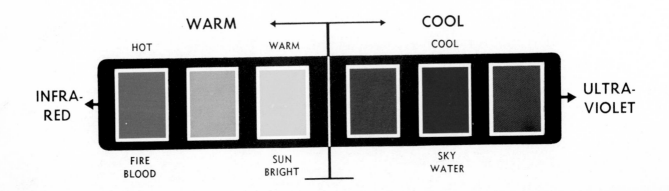

WARM

COOL

HOT

WARM

COOL

INFRA-RED

ULTRA-VIOLET

FIRE
BLOOD

SUN
BRIGHT

SKY
WATER

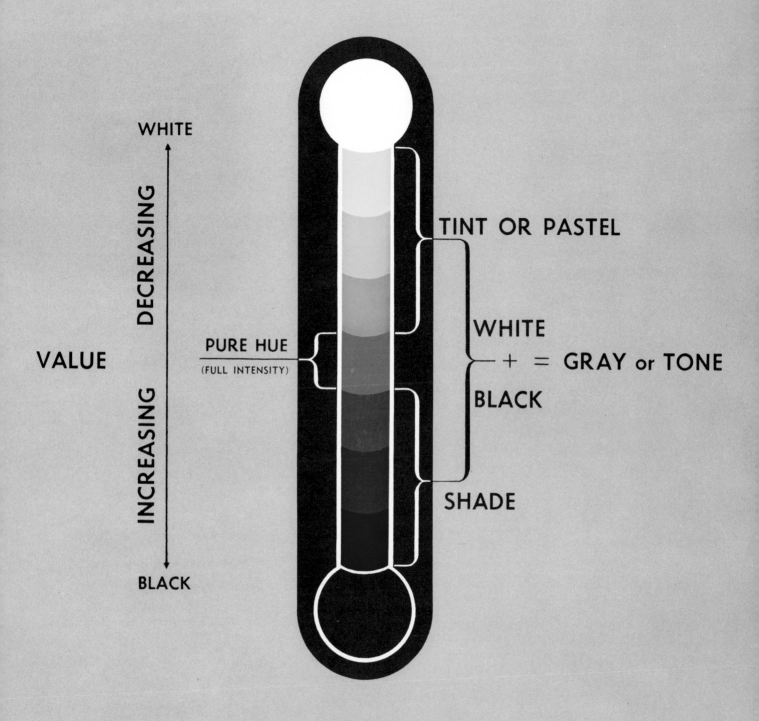

WHITE

VALUE

DECREASING

INCREASING

BLACK

PURE HUE
(FULL INTENSITY)

TINT OR PASTEL

WHITE
+ = GRAY or TONE
BLACK

SHADE

PLATE 96

BENZ COLOR BAROMETER

makes a blue-violet. The tertiary colors are formed by varying amounts of secondary colors.

The primary and secondary colors compose the color spectrum. They are the colors seen when light is refracted through a prism and subdivided into its seven component parts or when sunlight passes through the moisture in the air to form a rainbow.

All colors as seen by the eye are composed of light waves of varying wave lengths, each wave length producing its characteristic color. When light contacts an object, some of the wave lengths are reflected back to the eye and others are absorbed. Reflected wave lengths are the ones that enable us to see. An object appears red only because the red wave lengths are reflected to the eye and all other wave lengths are absorbed. If a red object were to be illuminated by a green light it would appear black, since all wave lengths (in this case only green) are absorbed and none can be reflected.

By placing colors of the spectrum in their proper sequence in a straight line, the degree of warmth and coolness of each color may be illustrated graphically. In the color blocks (Plate 95) of the same size we see that the warm colors advance and seem larger while the cool colors recede and appear smaller.

Red, which is first in the sequence, looks like blood or fire and is, therefore, a warm color. The excitement caused by fire or blood causes the heart to beat faster and naturally warms a person. Yellow, third in the sequence, is the color of the sun. It, too, is warm and brilliant. Orange, a mixture of two warm hues, red and yellow, is also warm. Blue, fifth in the spectrum, is a cool, receding color. It supplies a mental image of deep water and a cool limitless sky. If blue is mixed with yellow, cool green results. It is comparatively cool because of its blue parent.

Violet, a mixture of red and blue, may be either warm or cool, depending on whether the warm red or cool blue predominates.

NEUTRAL COLORS

Black, white, and gray are rarely found in nature, although they can be easily produced artificially by combining pigments. The combination of black and white gives gray. Gray is also produced when the three primary colors are mixed together. This is important to remember, for a garish combination can be subdued when using the complement of a color — a gray impression is the result when seen by the eye. The result of mixing a color with its complement is a muted color.

Although black and white do not appear in the spectrum, they are available in pigments and are very useful. Neither pure white nor black flowers appear in nature. "White" flowers have a green, yellow, or blue cast. "Black" flowers are of dark hues of red, purple, or brown, closely resembling black.

Black and white are used to change the value or tonal quality of a color. White lessens color value, making it lighter. Black increases color value making hues darker and adding depth. Mixing a hue with either alters the tonal value of a color.

White, black, and gray are useful. A white background blends colors and harmonizes hues. Pastels harmonize well because of the large quantity of white they contain. To blend two colors that appear to "fight," mix the two in the mind's eye. Mix white with this resulting color to get the pastel. This pastel will blend the two colors and supply the "go-between" or transition that is needed.

Light objects exhibit greater reflective quality and thus are cooler than the dark objects. Black, since it absorbs light rays, increases the brilliancy of red, blue, yellow, orange, and eliminates violet. Shadow box displays and the insides of florists' refrigerators are often painted black so that light will be absorbed rather than blend the flowers together. This black background appears to make flowers stand out as individual groups. Since light contains radiant energy (heat), the absorption of such light rays causes cut flowers

199

of dark colors to have a shorter life than lighter ones. Likewise, dark colored clothing is suited for Winter wear; light colored for Summer.

The combination of floral colors with fabrics often results in unequal light reflecting qualities. Flowers are somewhat translucent and reflective while fabrics are opaque and absorb light more readily.

DEFINITION OF TERMS

The following terms and definitions present the background necessary before color harmony can be clearly understood and used to advantage in all art forms.

COLOR HARMONY — the various usable or pleasing combinations of color (hue).

HUE — a particular color. Red, yellow and green are hues, regardless of the quantity of black or white they may contain. A dark red, maroon, medium red, and light red (pastel) are of the same color family.

CHROMA — the purity of a color, determined by its degree of freedom from white or gray; color intensity.

INTENSITY-CHROMA—pure hue, undiluted with white or black. Very little intensity-chroma is found in nature. Plant materials have mixtures of other hues in their composition. Although some flowers appear to have pure chroma it is the translucent quality, cell moisture, chlorophyl, and type of illumination that varies their true color.

VALUE — is the term used to designate the lightness or darkness of a hue. Neutral pigments change the value of a color. White lessens the value, making a hue lighter, and black increases the value, making the hue darker. The values of red, for example, range from light pink to dark maroon.

TINT — is any color to which white has been added, e.g., red plus white becomes pink, etc. Tints (pastels) are delicate and feminine.

SHADE — is a color to which black has been added, e.g., maroon is red with the addition of black.

200

TONE — is a color grayed by its complement or the addition of gray.

Review these terms collectively and study Plate 96. Color is called a hue. A hue in its pure, brilliant form is intensity chroma. When chroma is weakened with white, it becomes a tint or pastel. When chroma is strengthened with black, it gains in value and is called a shade. A color (hue) with a gray cast is a tone. It is readily understood from these definitions why black and white are considered neutral and used to vary the value of colors. They change the tonal quality of colors, but not their chroma or position on the spectrum or color wheel.

There are no ugly colors. It is improper use or placement of color that makes a color objectionable. Personal likes and dislikes are caused by first, nervous reaction, and second, educational value.

"Seeing color" is the impulse created by light reflected to the eye — this stimulus is transmitted by nerves to the brain where it registers color. Since this is true — and no two people have like nervous systems — we all react to color differently. We "see" color differently.

"Education" used here is the result of associational, psychological, and school training and the area in which a person lives. The associational and psychological aspects of color influence a person's choice and appreciation of color harmony. Contemporary use of color eliminates such fixations by placing importance on the sensuous impact of color. Personality traits greatly influence color preferences.

COLOR PROPERTIES

Scientists report that each hue has a different focal length; hence, some colors seem to advance, others recede. The noted painter, Cézanne, employed this property of color. Since the eye must adjust itself to each color, three dimensional illusion can be created. Poorly mixed colors or combinations cause nervous, jumpy feelings since the eye must constantly adjust itself to various focal lengths. Another problem in color harmony is created by the eye automatically noting the complement of a color just registered. This is called "after-image."

The eye sees colors in pairs. If the eye is looking at a strong red object, the after-image will be the complementary color, green. The three primary colors are thus seen. Complementary combinations are the least tiring and most pleasing. Radiant, luminous effects are produced by the juxtaposition of complementary colors. In theatrical stage settings the colored lights used produce shadows complementary to the main color. In a monochromatic combination, the eye is led smoothly through a gradation of tints and shades of one primary color and the eye has a minimum of adjustments to make. This will become monotonous unless the material has strong character. In an analogous scheme, the gradation is smooth due to the use of one primary hue relating the combination. Dominance of a strong color is important in this combination.

Advancing colors (red) or strong intensity (pure chroma) colors become trying when used profusely. As accent colors they are excellent. For gala occasions strong color is needed to create excitement, provided the affair is for a short time and not to be lived with for days.

In color harmony, texture plays an important part — it varies color perception. The smooth, shiny surface of the anthurium is quite different from the waxy appearance of a gardenia or the quality of a rose or carnation, even though each flower may be of same hue and value. Grayed colors often have a tweedy appearance, while colors that have black added may have a muddy appearance. Browns imply a rustic feeling that tends toward a coarse texture resulting in a masculine quality. The same material in pale pink or light blue gives a delicate, feminine feeling.

When working with color harmony, if there is doubt as to the true color of a flower or object, place it next to the primary color (full chroma) which predominates in the flower or near the strongest color of the materials to be used with the flower. The comparison will give the true color perception. If a red rose is placed near true red it will be obvious whether the rose tends toward blue or yellow. The red rose in its natural setting in the garden will be bright; however, placed in a room decorated in red it will lose its brilliancy and fade into the background.

EMOTIONAL RESPONSE

With the various terms and characteristics used to describe colors firmly in mind, consider the emotional response to color. Color cannot be generalized even though the language of color (response) is universal and most people of a given race react similarly. In the United States color has double meanings — either positive or negative.

YELLOW — when positive is cheerful and has the power, like sunshine, to dispel gloom. Those who have spent the winters in the cold gray North know the thrill of the first yellow crocus and the daffodils in bloom. Nature uses this hue to announce Spring. A word of warning — too much yellow becomes blinding, repeats and builds up its brilliance. Use a shade to subdue its intensity. Its negative meaning is cowardice or weakness.

RED, used positively, is a stimulating, exciting color. It has vitality and warmth. Red is aggressive and attacks. Here, also, use red with caution. When decorating a long room that you wish to fore-shorten, use red at the far end. Nature has toned down most natural reds so that they do not have full intensity (some red roses have a blue cast). Valentine reds have this blue cast, while reds used for Christmas are cardinal in that they lean toward yellow. Christmas red is exciting, joyful, and produces a festive mood. Red used negatively denotes anger, danger and disgrace.

Positive BLUE is a pleasing color; it is quiet, cool, and retiring. Blue has the quality of dignity and formality and is almost universal in its appeal. Blue is most attractive when seen by natural lighting; with artificial illumination it takes on a gray-purplish cast. Its receding quality suggests depth. When decorating a room, use blue to increase its size rather than to foreshorten it. Negative blue connotes depression, melancholy, timidity, and fright.

ORANGE is not as bright as yellow or as aggressive as red, but positively it is warm and has strong decorative value. Shadowy places such as hallways respond well to orange, or use it to advantage deep within an arrangement. Tints of orange — peach and flesh — may be used lavishly. Such tints are flattering to most skin tones. Orange has the negative, ghost-like connotation since it is well established with black and is used at Halloween. It is associated with the Souls in purgatory. It often means caution and grief.

GREEN is nature's favorite. It has both the cheerfulness of yellow and the coolness of blue. It counteracts the effects of heat and the brightness of sun. It is restful and is used in the abatement of excitement (the opposite of red). Green is the color of safety and the olive branch of peace. Negative green, however, means unripe, nausea, envy and poison.

VIOLET is a shadowy color, and may either be warm or cool, depending upon the percentage of red and blue in its makeup. The darker violets are solemn, dignified, and regal. The lighter tints are feminine. It is the only "shade" used at Easter time; all other colors used at this time are pastels. It denotes the royalty of Christ and the solemnity of the Easter service. Use violet only when there is strong natural light available, near windows or with bright backgrounds. Negatively it means melancholy and age.

With basic characteristics of color in mind, and a working knowledge of the terms used to describe them, *Free Form—Interpretive Design* takes on new significance — approach it with assurance.

204

COLOR HARMONY

A monochromatic color scheme is composed entirely of one hue (mono meaning one and chromatic meaning color). The hue remains constant but its value changes up or down the scale — tints, shades and tones of one hue are used. One value must predominate for interest. A design will become monotonous unless the materials have strong character in form and texture. Color gradations must be used with care with the strongest value and striking form placed at the center of interest. An arrangement of pink carnations and pink roses would be harmonious in color, yet greater interest is gained by changing to light pink snapdragons with either dark pink roses or carnations. Here the form and texture of the flowers, as well as the color value changes.

Symphonic Browns, Plate 2, moves like a symphony of tonal values as a theme in music weaves its pattern. The introduction of the green note in the vase and the one hosta leaf is a counterpoint to the major melody (color). The over-all minor chord is definitely stated in the quiet, though clear color of the Burmese ginger flower and accessories.

ANALOGOUS HARMONY is achieved through the use of three or more hues in sequence on the chart, with only one being a primary color. An analogous scheme attains its harmony by having the colors related to each other by a common parent. The parent color (primary red, blue, or yellow) predominates over the other hues. Use analogous harmony to produce a mood or seasonal effect — as yellow, orange, and brown suggest the colors of Fall.

The analogous color sequence in Plate 97, *Gin Jug*, gains distinction by its subtle graduation of tonal values. The tawny, brown tones of aspidistra and container are in perfect harmony of both color and texture which suggest this combination. Yellow, the pri-

PLATE 97
Gin Jug

Distinction is gained by subtle gradation of tonal values. Tawny brown aspidistra foliage and container are in perfect analogous color. Yellow, the primary color in the roses, carries the eye into the fruit of yellow and green. Darker green foliage provides the shades to act as a transition to the figurine and walnut base.

205

mary color, in the roses carries the eye in to the kumquat fruit of yellow and green. The brilliancy of yellow gives life and zest, preventing any monotony that may occur. Darker green foliage provides shade to act as a transition to the figurine and walnut base. Analogous color schemes require a smooth transition from one hue to the other in order to readily note the sequence. It is similar to the technique of flowing water colors one into the other.

The COMPLEMENTARY color scheme is a combination of hues in strong contrast. They are unrelated opposites on the color chart. Combination of complementary hues completes the three basic colors thus giving good color balance. Red and green are complementary — green furnishes the blue and yellow with the opposite red. Since the eye tends to produce an "after-image" (the complement of a color just seen), arrangements using this scheme are the most pleasing and the least tiring.

The addition of a color's complement tends to control the intensity of the strong hues. A brilliant red flower in a garden with its background of green foliage is vibrant, but when brought into a room decorated in red and related warm colors (where light is less intense or artificial) it will appear less brilliant and blend into the background.

Dramatic emphasis can be gained through the combination of intense values of chroma. In such cases, one color intensifies the other. The complementary combination is vibrant and expresses life and growth. Generally, for everyday use the most effective complementary harmonies are achieved by using a greater percentage of cool colors than warm colors, just as nature does by combining cool green leaves with warm red berries of holly. In Plate 98, *Hawaiian Memories*, vibrant flame ginger blossoms are held in control by the inter-

206

esting arrangement of dark green foliage radiating outward. The greater amount of green is needed to subdue the brilliancy of the red. One accents the other. Chartreuse bois d'arc apples are a transitional note of green that is needed between two main colors. The brown-green of the pineapples would be the resulting color by mixing all the colors together in the composition.

TRIAD is another interesting color scheme commonly used. It is the combination of three hues equally spaced on the color chart. By revolving the triangle on the chart, its three points will always indicate harmonizing colors.

COLOR RECIPE — *Percentage scale*

Color balance is as important in design as is the balancing of ingredients in making a cake. Too much of one element will spoil the whole. Call the correct color proportion a "recipe" or "percentage scale." Learning color value will aid greatly in achieving variety and creating color rhythm. A few color balance principles help.

Balance:

> Use the strong chroma — vivid value to the darker values in the center or focus, and the weaker (pastels) to the outside.

Proportion:

> The more dominant the color the less it is used. Like spices in cooking — a little will aid greatly — too much will spoil the dish.

Interest:

> Dominance and transition will be gained by the percentages and rhythm created by the variation in amounts.

The following percentages will be an invaluable guide to use in achieving color balance to add variety and interest to an arrangement and create color rhythm:

> 50-75% of a tint
> 10-15% of strong chroma (intensity)
> 15-25% of a shade (or dark tone)

An arrangement of pink snapdragons (tint) combined with rich pink roses (intensity) or a grouping of brightly colored flowers

PLATE 98
Hawaiian Memories

Vibrant flame ginger blossoms contrasts with the interesting parabolic arc of radiating dark green foliage. Chartreuse bois d'arc apples and greenish brown pineapples add a transitional note of color harmony.

and deep blue iris (shade) illustrates the percentages combined to achieve color balance.

Apply the percentages suggested to the selection of flowers for a corsage to complement a dress. If the dress is primarily a tint, the flowers could furnish the shade or intense color, with the ribbon completing the alternate color in the percentage chart.

GENERAL SUGGESTIONS

1. Tints are cooler and tend to harmonize in most combinations. Since the original hue has been lessened in value by the addition of white, tints may be used lavishly.

2. Shades are darker and heavy in visual weight. They are used to reduce general intensity of color combinations.

3. To subdue the intensity of a hue using pigments, use its complement. This has a neutralizing effect.

4. Tones, hues to which gray has been added, may be either light or dark and used as tints or shades.

5. Group colors, letting one flow into the other to produce rhythm in color harmony. Do not spot color around as it produces a salt and pepper effect. Have a definite pattern for each color.

6. Choose intense, vivid colors for focal points. The colors here must be stronger than elsewhere in the design.

7. When combining colors, change the value of each color to avoid monotony. Only one hue should dominate.

8. Use intense colors for dramatic combinations. They express activity and are appropriate for joyous occasions.

9. To create a dainty, feminine arrangement, use a combination of tints.

10. Remember that blues and yellows become less intense under artificial light. Blue may become purplish-gray; light yellow may fade entirely. If blue is to be used at night, select one on the purple side containing some red. The advancing quality of red tends to remove the gray cast.

11. Red, and any of its derivatives, shows up normally under artificial light because of its advancing quality.

12. Because of the diverging quality of warm colors, size appears larger than the same quantity of a cool, receding color.

13. Warm, advancing colors unify an arrangement and are seen first by the viewer.

14. Cool colors supply depth and create a third dimensional feeling in an arrangement.

208

Chapter VI

Containers

Today's mode of living has completely changed the idea concerning the word "container." Traditionally the container was a utilitarian receptacle for holding something (either liquids, grains, fruit, or flowers) or as an object of art (Wedgewood, Dresden, or Sevres porcelain). Interior trends and new concepts of design have opened unlimited vistas in the search for so-called "containers." There is freedom of choice and unrestricted scope as to what constitutes a container. The traditional and utilitarian type are familiar; they are seen everywhere. But the use of the unusual, free form, even to the unique containers that cause excitement, is what contemporary decor demands. As in Plate 72, *Tropical Mobile,* such a container, which was designed for a tropical pool in the author's home, is provocative. Orchid culture is his hobby. These flowers usually speak of formality, which characteristic makes them somewhat limited in use. This unique mobile has an orchid tube, countersunk in the manzanita wood, which supplies water for the flowers. Even the most elegant, formal Cattleya or the humble informal specie orchid of the spray variety feels at home in its native setting in such a "container." It is a conversation piece which brings joy to all.

The container is an integral part of any flower arrangement. It is the starting point or foundation on which the three-dimensional picture is built. Keep in mind that one creating a floral picture with plant materials is comparable to a painter using oils, a sculptor using stone or clay, or an artist in other fields using his medium to create.

What kind of a container is just right? Study the word *"Suitability."* It is a big word in floral art and covers a multitude of conditions. Appropriateness and suitability are two prerequisites that most fulfull the requirements. Its suitability contributes to the proper mental attitudes toward accomplishing the final results. An understanding of its meaning will clear many problems arising in the selection of this important object. A container for the home, garden club show, or other display, depends on its suitability. Picture the container in use before making a choice. Recall the number of places in the home where flowers are enjoyed and the type or kind of flowers grown or purchased, then buy to suit the needs. Gradually add to this collection as proficiency in floral art increases. A really "good" container is one that is a pleasure to use; it fits well into its surroundings and lends itself to various types of designs. Practical value is vital; price is not a criterion. There is great satisfaction in possessing the right container. One which does not blend becomes a problem and causes discontent; the floral picture appears to be "ill at ease" when it is used. Impulse buying of a beautiful container that strikes a person's fancy or the lovely impractical gift chosen without the consideration of the arranger's preference should be eliminated.

The florist who is sending flowers to a hospital, or making a general gift arrangement, chooses a container that serves a utilitarian purpose, that of holding the flowers and water. The general florist arrangement (when not ordered for a specific location in a home or definite purpose) is a unit within itself. Its destination or placement in a room does not influence the design.

Shape, size, color, texture, and associational value must be considered. Often the artistic value, distinction, or individuality of a design hinges on the selection of the container. There are no rules or limitations in the choice. Let good taste, appropriateness, and common sense guide. A great part of the interest and leisure fun of flower arranging lies in the challenge and search for the container and the problem it presents. In Plate 42, *Danish Modern Hen*; Plate 2, *Symphonic Browns*; and Plate 55, *Motion in Space*, the container was a challenge; each presented a special problem and thereby created interest.

Various objects converted into containers, such as lamp bases, imported objects of antiquity, candlesticks, cookie jars, hollowed driftwood, or palm spathes, lend the note of individuality and distinction sometimes needed in an arrangement. Americans have no qualms about converting a utensil or any other object to suit their needs; however, the Orientals are held by tradition and by their respect to the Masters. They feel that only those containers made for floral arrangements can be used for such. In Plate 27, *Buddhist Prayer Gong*, the use of the ritual prayer gong in this floral arrangement would be considered a sacrilege to the Oriental; however, the Americans feel that a Far Eastern atmosphere is established by its use.

Traditional or conventional design never allows a container to dominate a composition. The flowers, the container, and the decor of the room must complement each other. If a container competes with the flowers, it appears to dominate and the value of the floral composition is lessened. When the transitional relationship between parts is not smooth the eyes dwell on the container. Containers must not "steal the show" in conventional designing, but may be the featured part in contemporary design. A simple, tailored-to-fit, unadorned container will often be more effective than the ornate, highly decorative pieces. Containers with good, simple design, curved or straight line, and of muted color, will be the most popular ones.

In *Free Form—Interpretive Design,* it may be the container that is featured. In such cases all materials are subordinated to accent the intrinsic value of this object. Plate 55, *Motion in Space;* Plate 42, *Danish Modern Hen;* Plate 2, *Symphonic Browns.*

Associational value plays a great part in floral designing in portraying floral composition. A classic urn is immediately associated with the Empire period or French or Italian Renaissance, as in Plate 15, *Florentine Elegance* and Plate 17, *A Sèvres Porcelain.* Iron kettles, bean pots, and other culinary utensils are reminiscent of the Early American period and often imply casual living. A pumpkin container establishes a Fall idea for Thanksgiving or Halloween. Half of a fresh watermelon used as a "bowl" with flowers arranged in it will be suitable for a patio party. Free form vases or bowls that are angular and strong in color or texture are associated with contemporary design. Thus the mood and emotional response to a design may be established by featuring a container. It can create atmosphere through association, complete harmony and unify the composition.

Undesirable containers are those that either present a problem of balance or create a second center of interest. Similarly, the container is also undesirable that has a large mouth opening and decreases in size toward the bottom with no additional base added. This type will appear too heavy when the flowers are placed in it and will create an uneasy feeling. Visual balance as well as mechanical balance is lost. This arrangement will have the tendency to fall forward.

The *Weight* of the container, either actual weight (e.g., pottery, brass, iron, or bronze), or the apparent visual weight (e.g., dark colors and heavy texture), affects the proportion of the arrangement to the size of the container. Pottery gives the appearance of having more weight than fine china. Pewter, iron and bronze are heavier in actual weight than pottery or crystal of the same shape. Also the color of a container will change its visual weight in appearance, e.g., a dark receptacle equal in size and shape to a light colored one will appear heavier.

In a heavy container of either pottery, metal, or earthenware, one can exceed the standard proportion of 1½:1 ratio. When weight alone is considered, a higher arrangement, or a larger quantity of blossoms, can be used in such a heavy container, thus exceeding the proportion. Good judgment guides in this case. Clear, fine quality crystal is lighter than thick etched glass. The fine quality of bone china and clear crystal, due to their excellent texture, will hold a design within the limits of the accepted proportions of 1½:1.

The *Lines* of the container may often dictate the lines of the arrangement thus determining the floral pattern. Unity is apparent in such instances. Containers with dominant lines impose certain restrictions (requirements) on the arranger as in Plate 42, *Danish Modern Hen;* this ceramic piece forces one to follow its dictates and with pleasure. This is also true in Plate 73, *Driftwood Serpent;* the driftwood piece practically tells the arranger what is to be developed in the design. By following these lines suggested by the container, logical movement and rhythm are created; the arrangement becomes alive with motion.

When a water pitcher is used as a container, we visualize the flow of liquid over the lip. This curved line establishes the line of the flower arrangement. The flowers should follow the direction indicated by the lip, thus completing the mental picture which the mind's eye formulates on seeing this type of receptacle. The heavier portion of the arrangement will be toward the side of the handle. If a focal point is developed, it is located near the spot where the handle joins the upper rim of the

PLATE 99 *Nautilus Pitcher*

212

Birds of Paradise in Flight PLATE 100

PLATE 99

Nautilus Pitcher

Pink snapdragons continue the line of the floral composition dictated by the pitcher. Roses in tones of medium pink to deep rose pink with ranunculi blossoms furnish the round flower forms for mass. The handle has line value and is therefore visible.

PLATE 100

Birds of Paradise in Flight

Motion in the floral forms blend perfectly with the container. The bracts of the strelitzia are the shape of the upper rim of the pitcher and continue this directional motion. The handle is free of materials to lend full support to the flow line.

container. In Plate 64, *Arrested Motion*; Plate 99, *Nautilus Pitcher*; and Plate 100, *Birds-of-paradise in Flight*, we see interesting varieties of arrangements in pitchers. The stylized colt, Plate 64, *Arrested Motion*, checks the motion expressed in the rapid movement of the birds-of-paradise. The flowers carry forward the motion established by the lip of the container. To add force to this movement the one leaf repeats the body lines of the pitcher and counteracts the weight of the figurine. The contemporary composition has no focal point as in traditional design which is evident in Plate 99.

In Plate 99, *Nautilus Pitcher*, traditional in style, the definite lines are as demanding as those of the contemporary Danish container, but their flowing, graceful curves are suggestive of compatible floral material. The design is in the conventional line mass formation inherited from the European culture. The pink snapdragons so repeat the lines and segmented shape of the bluish-gray container, that they, too, are the perfect complement

to develop the floral pattern. The snapdragons set the framework in which the mass flowers are arranged. A definite focal area is announced in the opened dark red roses, tying the whole together. The other flowers are rose-pink ranunculi and roses with daffodils and tulips in contrast. Note the force of line developed in the tallest snapdragon followed by a second, through a rose then into the low, fully developed snapdragon, forming a lazy "S" curve through the composition. The handle is integrated into the design as part of the floral pattern and not freely exposed as in the two examples above. (Compare this composition to the *Danish Modern Hen*, Plate 42, for compatible materials.)

Plate 100, *Birds-of-paradise in Flight*, again the strelitzia flowers give motion to the logical flow of line from the lip of the pitcher. The tritoma blossoms form a secondary line, the lower two emphasizing the handle while the upper one reinforces the main flowers. The handle is clearly visible which adds interest to the design.

213

The semi-focal point is developed by the use of the grapes which carry the eye to the fruit in the wicker tray. Note that the three bananas appear to tie in with the three birds-of-paradise and tritoma. The dark grapes are used to continue the downward line which originated with the white grapes flowing from the pitcher. Here are two main forces in contrast,—the upper force of flowers and downward pull of the grapes working in harmony. Plate 101, *Colonial Pitcher*, design also returns to the traditional, however, the flow of line is the same. The shape of the container governs in these two arrangements, determining the main lines. For the children: A miniature wash bowl and pitcher is spilling over with floribunda roses that carry the eye to the little lamb figurine. Even though all round (mass) flowers are used, the flow of line from the lip of the pitcher is developed. The more opened flowers are used in the focal area to give weight. Line suggested by the container rules the composition. In Plate 51, *Sea Horse*, the novelty container of ultramarine blue sets the lines developed by the rich

yellow tulips. The curve of the top blossom with its foliage is perfect in line harmony. The sea horse shows alertness in its carriage and the placement of this tulip enhances this quality. The reflexed petals of the two central flowers give weight to the design. Hyacinth-flowered candytuft (filler flowers) give textural contrast to the smooth ceramic piece and tulips. The informality of this design is relaxing, and the arrangement may be used on the sun porch of the home or in the family room.

Cornucopias and nautilus sea shells also have demanding lines when used as containers. The line formed from the tip of the horn to the opening, establishes the line pattern. The cornucopia container suggests overflowing harvest. This idea should be developed with fruits and flowers used in abundance. The conformation of the sea shell suggests motion of the line pattern.

Low, horizontal containers are more informal than tall, vertical stem-ware such as compotes and pedestal bowls, therefore, they lend themselves to informal floral patterns. Low, shallow bowls provide excellent containers for asymmetrical or crescent designs, (Plate 62, *Crescent Callas*). Tall containers show strength and impart a virile feeling that commands attention as in Plate 97, *Gin Jug*. Classic urns of alabaster and bronze pedestal bowls are formal in feeling and association which suggests formal floral patterns.

Color plays an important part in container selection. It must either blend or contrast with the floral material or with the decor of the room. When a container blends with main flowers it will tend to fade into the background harmoniously; or if there is a contrast, the container will add emphasis to the design. The latter case will require careful handling. When the colors of the container contrast with plant materials, each must have a definite part in the scheme, as in Plate 97, *Gin Jug*, which blends, or Plate 36, *Modern Madonna*, which contrasts.

The substance and finish of the container with its color provide *textural* quality. This quality influences the selection of flowers. When the flowers are at hand and the container is to be selected, it must be fitted to the flowers and the decor of the room. For example, sweet peas seem lost and uncomfortable when arranged in a rough textured, pottery bowl and placed in a room of masculine, tweedy decor. The elements of texture discussed in the chapter on *Principles* apply to containers also.

Clear crystal containers are fascinating to use and a challenge to the designer. Unusual design effects can be displayed, presenting dramatic conversation arrangements. During the Victorian era, glass domes were popular for dried flower arrangements. A somewhat similar effect is obtained when designing within clear crystal containers. Today, there are a great number of clear glass containers available, e.g., hurricane globes, brandy snifters, rectangular blocks, etc. They are more interesting when the floral design is arranged within the container. In Plate 34, *Serenity*, the whole composition and ethereal feeling is enhanced by the inclosure of

the container. The design seems to be set apart from worldly existence. This simple, but magnificent, arrangement is in a serene setting because of the clear glass hurricane globe. The crescent pattern was selected to bring in an element of the universe—the new moon symbolizes Heaven. Soft pink carnations caress the madonna, expressive of the delicacy in theme, while deep red roses give a firm foundation and are symbolic of love. Lycopodium foliage blends with texture and quality of crystal. In Plate 52, *Oriental Occult Balance*, the whole composition is dependent on the clear crystal container for distinction. The play of textures and rhythmic movement would be broken if designed in any other type container.

Crystal or glassware elaborately ornamented with frills and furbelows (Venetian, Italian, etc.) do not usually blend with flowers. They demand too much attention thus detracting from the flowers and themselves.

Colored glass is most pleasing when it is used near a source of light which blends its color with the flowers. The translucent quality of flowers and of glass gives a sparkling effect to the composition. Sunny windows or reflecting mirrors give this needed light.

Novelty containers or ones with decorative pictures are always popular when the occasion demands, e.g., hearts for Valentine's Day, bride and groom for weddings, animals for circus parties. Interest and enthusiasm are as high with adults as with children. Novelties can be used to set the theme for an occasion. In planning a flower arrangement, each detail must be coordinated and harmonious with flowers and setting. The idea expressed in containers must be suitable. When planning a festive occasion, select one of the units for a dominant feature and subordinate all other details. Study the characteristics of this type container, the meaning it portrays, its design features, and then fit the flowers and foliage to emphasize these characteristics. The feature has value of its own, and this must be clearly visible when the design is completed. When flowers cover the novelty, its value is lost. The flowers and novelty must be a single unit. If the flowers arise from it in a volcanic effect, two separate units are created.

ACCESSORIES

Accessories are accent objects or necessary items for the completion of a harmonious composition. Figurines, backgrounds, driftwood, dried materials, mirrors, fruit, etc., are included in this category. They add interest to the designs and more or less set the "stage." A note of authenticity is given the composition by their use. Any accessory should stimulate the imagination. It should tell a story, set the mood or complete the idea. It must be an integral part and harmonize in all aspects. Use restraint in the choice of accent materials; if they do not contribute full value, leave them out. Avoid stereotyped, monotonous use of figurines; dullness is imparted when they are over-used; originality is destroyed.

An accessory may often supply a needed element, e. g., add weight for balance, accent line, or give necessary color, etc. In Plate 52, *Occult Balance* the figurine is needed to complete balance. The weight of the blossoms on the right is counterbalanced by interest and weight in the figurine to the left. The three curves of the figure repeat the three curves in the tritomas which are united by the vertical line formed by the three Fuji mums. Only an Oriental figurine could be used to harmonize with the blossoms which are Oriental in origin. Another interesting feature of this design is that the lines of the figurine and the lines of the tritomas flow in opposite directions. This is quite unusual for line generally follows the main lines of the composition. If this design is sketched on paper, one would immediately recognize the curving roof of the pagodas of Japan in the up-turned lines of flowers and figure.

In Occidental floral design the definition of

PLATE 102
Autumn Call

Fall migration is definitely implied by the duck in flight. On this wall tray design, a huntsman's imagination is given full freedom by the accessories.

the historical period is established by the use of accessory materials, thus creating the proper atmosphere. For example in Plate 23, *Victorian Shadow Box*, the fan and cluster of violets blend beautifully with the Victorian vase which is ornamented with pictures of violets and accents of gold. The background is deep purple velvet adding to the lavishness of the period. This composition is enhanced by the beaded gold-leafed frame. A note of authenticity is given this Victorian design through the use of the accessory items and background; they more or less set the stage for the presentation of the floral arrangement. Also in Plate 11 the greatly admired statue, Venus de Milo, not only suggests the historical period but it stimulates the imagination. It tells the story of Grecian splendor which inspired the creation of this floral composition.

An accessory should carry a message, clearly stating the theme being developed. In Plate 102, *Autumn Call*, the message of Fall migration is definitely implied by the ducks in flight. A huntsman's imagination is given full freedom. This story is carefully told by accessories; without them the composition would lack meaning. Intimacy in the scene is created by the nearness of the large bird; the one on the edge of the basket to the right suggests the

PLATE 103

Marshland

Motion of the ducks flying out
of marshlands create a secondary
line that is swift and strong. Accessories are featured.

escape from man's pursuit, and the third duck is used behind the materials, high in the composition, to create a feeling of distance by perspective lines converging in infinity.

Those accessories having definite lines add motion; it is important that these lines follow the pattern set by the flowers. They must either flow with the motion in the arrangement or carry the eye back into the design. Should a round mirror be used, the main lines follow the edges suggesting circular motion. Excellent examples are found in Plates 62 and 63, where the lines flow in this circular path. Either of these arrangements could be used with a round mirror or tray. In Figure 8 the lines of both flower composition and figurine complement each other. However, should the figurine be placed outside of the design, another accessory with lines flowing in opposite direction would be needed. Figure 8 and Plate 26 show how the line of the accessory returns the eye to the floral composition.

In Plate 103 the motion of the ducks flying out of the asymmetrical arrangement creates a secondary line that is swift and strong. The ducks replace plant material and carry as much weight in the design by their interest value.

The accessory should feel "at home" in its place. Dry land objects do not care to be used in water nor do aquatic types like to be combined with cacti. In Plate 35 the Brahman bull is in his ideal setting; the ducks mentioned above also belong to their home in the marsh lands. In Plates 40, 62, and 63, the flower goddess can be used within the design for she is purposely placed on a pedestal with suggestive flowers and plants growing about her feet. She is clear of the water.

To secure a figurine, attach floral clay to its base and then press it firmly into position. An inverted pin frog will form a good base to raise a figurine to desired height. The base of the figurine generally should be level with the edge of the container when used inside the container.

BASES

Bases add importance to an arrangement. A base produces the same effect of completion to the composition as a frame contributes to a painting, a pedestal to a sculptured piece or the floor covering to a room. Careful selection will enhance the design and give dignity where only a commonplace feeling existed until the base was added. The base or pedestal may be considered a part of the container, as in Plate 55, or as an accessory to lend atmosphere, e. g., an Oriental carved wooden base, Plate 26. The base sets the arrangement apart from its surroundings. Oriental arrangements require an appropriate base for distinction. Plate 6, *Classical Ikenobo Aspidistra*, and Plate 7, *Summer — San-ju-giri*, require their respective bases to complete the composition, and too, traditional Japanese design demands these bases.

When weight is needed, it can be gained by the use of bases. They may be small Oriental tables, pedestals of classical designs, mirrored plaques, discs of various types, bamboo mats, segments of tree trunks or whatever the occasion dictates. Often an inverted bowl or vase will suffice as in Plate 58, *Contemporary Ikenobo*, where an inverted salad bowl is used.

A container which may have all prerequisites for a design but is too light in visual balance can be made satisfying by the addition of bases. This was true in Plate 1, where a second smaller square was needed under the chalice to add importance and weight. Also in Plate 56, the base supplied a foundation for the tall vertical arrangement.

Chapter VII

Care of Cut Flowers

Good habits formed in the care and handling of cut flowers pay dividends in longer flower life. Whether flowers are bought or grown, the basic rules of flower care must be observed. They represent a long investment in time and skill to bring them to their full beauty. Unless flowers serve their purpose and live their normal period of expectancy in an arrangement, all effort is lost. In corsages the life of a flower is much shorter than a flower in water. Regardless of its use the flower must be conditioned.

Flowers from the garden should be cut early in the morning or late in the evening when they are crisp and turgid with water. Give most stems a long, slanting cut with a sharp knife. Do not use scissors as they squeeze the ends of the stem together and hinder water intake. Use a meat tenderizer for crushing stems that require this practice (woody stems). After cutting or crushing, place them in deep water immediately and allow them time to absorb all the water possible before arranging. A few flowers can absorb water along their stems, or through their faces, but most flowers take water only through a cut at the base. This preserves their freshness and assures longer life. When flowers are received from the florist, if tied in bundles with wire, string, or rubber bands, these should be removed and the stems re-cut, before placing in storage containers. To cut a stem, hold the knife blade firmly in the hand, and with the thumb keeping the stem toward the blade; insert the blade slightly into the stem. The hand with the knife is pulled back while the hand holding the stem pushes outward. Do not try "peeling potatoes" in cutting a stem; this binds the knife blade. Some flowers are stubborn about water intake and require cutting under water, to prevent air bubbles blocking the flow of water.

Some flowers, e. g., zinnias, dahlias, stocks, asters, and marigolds, have foliage that decays quickly when submerged in water and creates offensive odor. In these cases the leaves should be stripped from the lower third of the stems. Other flowers have foliage that can withstand submerging. This group includes roses, carnations, and most bulbous-types such as gladioli, narcissi and tulips. Experiments have proven that the pH of water (pH symbol indicates acidity or alkalinity of liquid) affects the life of cut flowers. A pH of 7 is neutral. It has been proven in the Benz School of Floral Design that a few drops of sulphuric acid, mouth wash antiseptic (e. g., Listerine) or similar products will definitely aid in prolonging the life of cut flowers. This school uses Listerine; a cap full to approximately three gallons of water will be sufficient. When using sulphuric acid, five drops to ten gallons of water will suffice. Litmus paper is used for testing the pH. (Litmus — an organic dye that turns blue in alkalines and red in acids. It is used in the form of treated paper prepared chiefly in the Netherlands from certain lichens). The depth of water depends on the type of flowers. It is an excellent practice to allow flowers to absorb water for an hour or two before placing them in a refrigerator. After flowers have become turgid with water, they can be used in arrangements in shallow bowls without wilting. Flowers in bud form, e. g., roses, gladi-

219

oli, and Easter lilies, which must be developed rapidly should be placed in warm water in a warm room. If they show signs of wilting from this treatment, return them to water of room temperature.

Complete submersion for several hours or even overnight is recommended for flowers with large blossoms that tend to wilt easily. Poinsettias and hydrangeas benefit by this treatment. The length of time flowers should remain in a refrigerator depends on the type of flower and condition at the time of picking. This process is called hardening and the lasting quality of an arrangement depends upon its thoroughness. Flowers can be successfully stored for several weeks in the refrigerator if kept just above the freezing point (33°-35°) and protected from dehydration; e. g., roses, peonies, etc. Wrap them in foil or cellophane bags. Best temperatures range from 40°-50° + for normal refrigeration.

Soft blossoms such as stock cannot be submerged because the blossoms tend to become water logged and mildew develops.

Never place cut flowers in drafts, near radiators, sunny locations, or directly under an electric light. They transpire more rapidly than they can absorb water, which causes them to wilt.

CHEMICAL PRESERVATIVES

Scientists and laymen have been searching for that element or combination of chemicals which will prolong the life of cut flowers. There are many chemicals that are said to be beneficial and it is interesting to try them. It is much easier and more practical, however, to use the dependable commercial products on the market today which are excellent. Some flowers are greatly benefited by their use while others seem unaffected. These products may be purchased at retail florist's shops. Flower preservatives are a mixture of sugar, acidifiers to prevent bacterial growth, and a fungicide that kills fungi. A small amount of detergent added to the water in the container causes it to be absorbed more readily by the flower.

Containers and frogs should be thoroughly cleaned after each use with detergent and hot water. Fresh water (80° to 110°) is used each time for a new bunch of flowers. The container is cleaned to eliminate bacteria and other elements which clog the stems. Open neck containers for storage of flowers allow freer development of flowers and better circulation of cool moist air.

For foliage arrangements that will last for long periods of time it is well to use charcoal in the container to keep the water "sweet." Should water become cloudy, change it and rinse the charcoal and refill container.

The white water deposit in crystal containers can be removed by soaking the containers overnight in a strong solution of tea or vinegar. The tannic acid removes the alkaline deposit.

Special Treatments — Various types of flowers will respond rapidly and last longer if cut at the best stage of development. For those who like to experiment with cut flowers, a list of suggestions is given for time of cutting and use of various chemicals.

Amaryllis — ¾ to fully open. Add 1 tablespoon oil of peppermint per quart of water.

Anemones — ½ to fully open. Add ½ cup vinegar to 2 cups water.

Asters — ¾ to fully open. Add 1 teaspoon sugar to 1 quart water.

Azaleas — Buds to fully open, crush stems.

Callas — Buds to fully open. Add ½ cup vinegar to 2 quarts water.

Calendulas — Buds to fully open.

Camellias—Similar to pansies and violets, they respond to moisture on their petals and a high humidity. Placing dampened cotton or a paper towel over their faces and storing them in waxed boxes aids greatly.

Carnations—½ to fully open, break at joint for longer lasting quality. They last longer if they are placed in room temperature or even tepid water for several hours. Do not use cold water. Refrigeration and cold water sometimes cause them to "go to sleep." If the carnations are cut green, leave them out of the refrigerator for 24 hours or more; this greatly increases their size. Add 5 drops of oil of peppermint in 2 quarts of water, or ½ cup of boric acid in 1 gallon of water.

Chrysanthemums — ½ to fully open. Add 8 drops of oil of peppermint to 2 quarts water. Chrysanthemums should have their stems broken or crushed rather than cut. Those with hard woody stems sometimes will not absorb water. Break these under water to prevent any air bubbles forming. Chrysanthemums do not shatter normally. The dropping of petals is caused by improper handling or some other form of damage. To prevent further loss of petals, drop candle wax at point of injury (Figure 18).

Corsage Flowers—That have first been placed in water and hardened may be kept for long periods of time in the humid atmosphere of the vegetable hydrator in the refrigerator or in waxed boxes or cellophane bags.

Fig. 18 — *Melted candlewax is dropped at base of falling petals to correct damage and further loss of petals.*

Daffodils — ½ to fully open.

Dahlias — Full maturity — sear end of stems. Petals may be removed; the seed pod with calyx makes a lovely chartreuse "flower." 1 teaspoon of wood alcohol to 1 quart water, soak for two hours, then remove and place in fresh water.

Daisies — Fully opened. Add 8 drops of oil of peppermint to 1 quart water.

Day Lilies — ¾ to fully open.

Delphiniums — ¾ open; add 1 tablespoon wood alcohol to 1 quart water.

Easter Lilies — Either in bud stage or when partially open. Remove antlers, all pollen from lilies. The stain it leaves on clothing is difficult to remove.

Evergreens — Should be broken, or the ends crushed with a hammer, and charcoal added to the water. This makes for longer lasting arrangements and does away with offensive odors.

Gardenias — ¾ to fully open. They are similar to pansies and violets, they respond to moisture on their petals and high humidity. Placing dampened cotton or a paper towel over their faces and storing them in waxed boxes aids greatly.

Gerberas — ¾ to fully open.

Gladioli — When first flower begins to open.

Hydrangeas — Should have their stem ends seared with flame or dipped in boiling water immediately after cutting. (Figure 19). After this treatment completely submerge them in deep water for several hours or overnight. Add ½ cup vinegar to 2 quarts water.

Irises — When first bud is ready to open.

Larkspurs — ¾ to fully open. ½ teaspoon wood alcohol to 2 quarts of water for 1 hour.

Lilacs — ¾ to fully open. They should have their stems broken and should be stripped of all foliage but a few leaves nearest the flower head. This will help pull water up into the blossom, submerge for two hours if they begin to wilt.

Lilies-of-the-Valley — ¾ to fully open. They are greatly benefited by the use of a thin wax solution, or Merdisco (see plastic coating).

Marigolds — ¾ to fully open. Use a weak thin acid solution.

Peonies — Cut when full color is showing in the bud or when partially open, remove unnecessary foliage. Add 2 teaspoons sugar to 2 quarts of water.

Poinsettias — Should have their stem ends seared with flame or dipped in boiling water immediately after cutting (Figure 19). After this treatment, completely submerge in deep water for several hours. Yard grown poinsettias should have all unnecessary leaves removed two or three days in advance of cutting to allow scars to heal before cutting and searing.

Poppies — Should have their stem ends seared with flame or dipped in boiling water immediately after cutting (Figure 19). After this treatment, completely submerge in deep water for several hours.

Fig. 19 — *Searing ends of stems with milky juices prevents wilting. Use flame or boiling water. Protect foliage by wrapping the stems with newspaper.*

Roses — When the outer petals begin to open, cut with a sharp knife. There is no need to lose roses growing in the garden that are threatened by a freeze. Those showing color can be cut and stored. Seal the stems with melted paraffin. Roll in a damp paper towel, then wax paper. Store in a hydrator of the refrigerator. Such roses can be kept for six to eight weeks and then used in flower arrangements. Add 5 drops wood alcohol to 2 quarts water or 1 tablespoon powdered alum in 1 quart water.

Snapdragons — ¾ to fully open. Do not store near fruit. Add 3 tablespoons of baking soda to 2 quarts water.

Stocks — Last longer when the stems are crushed with a hammer. Damp stock blossoms will mildew rapidly and damage all flowers in a short time. To check the spread of mildew, remove infected blossoms and let dry air circulate through the good blossoms before placing them in the refrigerator.

Sweet Peas — ¾ to fully open. Snap stems from

vine by lifting them with the thumb and index finger while applying pressure to the rear of joint with the middle finger.

Tulips — ½ to fully open — wrap in newspaper and sink into water neck deep.

Violets — Remain fresh when they have moisture on their petals. Violets picked from the garden should be submerged in water for two or three hours and sprayed several times a day. Store in cellophane bags in the hydrator.

Water Lilies — Cut in bud stage just before opening. They naturally open and close with the rising and setting of the sun. To prevent closing, drop candle wax at the base of the petals. (Figure 20). The hardened wax will prop the petals open.

Wisteria — ¾ open in the evening. Add ¼ cup alcohol to 1 quart water.

Woody Stems — Blossoms of fruit trees, redbud, dogwood, lilac, etc., should have their stems crushed with a hammer, or scraped with a knife, or the bark peeled back to increase water absorption area. If

Fig. 20 — *Use candlewax at base of water lily petals to prevent closing.*

the branches are heavy with foliage, ½ or more of the leaves should be removed so they will not rob the blossoms of water. If foliage is removed from alternate places along a branch, its natural appearance will be maintained.

Zinnias — Fully opened — use acid in water.

Note: Do not store fruit (apples, bananas, avocados, lemons, etc.) in storage with flowers. These fruits give off ethylene gas which can cause sleepy carnations, petal drop of roses, tulips, and flower drop of snapdragons.

SPECIAL TREATMENT
PRESERVING CUT FLOWERS

1. GLYCERINE METHOD — To preserve foliage and also cause it to turn a rich brown, place fresh (crushed) stems in a solution of $\frac{1}{3}$ to $\frac{1}{2}$ glycerine and $\frac{2}{3}$ water. Allow 2 to 3 weeks for the branches to absorb this liquid. The foliage will be pliable and last for several years.

2. DRYING METHODS — Foliage and flowers may be dehydrated and retain much of their natural beauty. This material is cut at the proper stage of development to prevent disintegration. Most plant material should be gathered just before reaching maturity. Fall foliage will retain its color better if the branches are cut when the color begins to turn. A corner in the attic or basement, away from traffic and light (which causes color to fade) is a good place for drying materials. Dampness causes mildew preventing proper drying. Check material carefully before placing in storage. When flowers or foliage are to be pressed use several layers of newspaper and change frequently. Corrugated cardboard used between sections will allow air circulation. Heavy weights are used to apply pressure evenly. Allow several weeks for material to cure.

The foliage of flowers is removed. Group the flowers in small bunches and hang upside down. For special curves, secure the branches with pins on a stiff cardboard backing, then allow to dry. To curve or soften dried material, place it in warm water or give it a steam bath over a kettle or in the shower. Position the stem and let it dry in the preferred shape.

3. BOILING METHOD—Magnolia and ficus (rubber plant) foliage may be boiled in very soapy water to turn it white. It lasts a long time without disintegrating.

4. GLUEING — Plant material that sheds quickly may be preserved by dipping it in a weak solution of shellac. Cattails, artichokes, etc., are greatly benefitted by this method. They absorb the solution which seals (glues) the flower parts to the stem.

5. PLASTIC AND WAX COATING — Some flowers and accent foliage wilt quickly even when the stems are in water or worn in corsages. These may be covered with a plastic or wax coating which eliminates excessive transpiration. Their usefulness is prolonged several days.

Plastic coating may be purchased in pressurized cans and sprayed on the plant material. Or it may be purchased in small quantities ($\frac{1}{2}$ pints to gallons) and mixed with water according to directions on the container. There are two commercial products of this type, Merdisco and Miracle Mastic, that are excellent. Generally, 2 parts of water and one part of the plastic is used. Merdisco may be purchased in a milky white or a clear form. When using dark colored flowers, it is best to tint the water a darker color than the flower to eliminate any frosty appearance. This white film shows only on dark colored flowers. When glitter is being used, dust it on before the solution dries.

The author has used this method with great success. Flowers, e. g., camellias, lily-of-the-valley, phalaenopsis orchids have been used in flower shows without any evidence of the solution. These flowers mentioned lasted one week in excellent condition. The camellias in Plate 18 are eight days old. Merdisco was used.

Spray plastics from pressurized cans is clear. It is excellent to prevent wilting or shedding of dried materials, and most efficient for holding glitter. The backs of foliage can be sprayed to prevent curling.

Coating with floral wax has been found beneficial in keeping delicate flowers from wilting and in prolonging the life of the blossoms. Flowers to be waxed must be at room temperature and thoroughly dry. Do not remove flowers from refrigerator and wax immediately. Floral wax may be sprayed onto the foliage and blossoms with an atomizer without any thinning. In some cases a thinner solution of wax is more satisfactory. To dilute wax, use two parts wax to one part water and mix thoroughly with a rotary egg beater. This solution may be sprayed onto the flowers or the blossoms may be dipped and then drained of surplus wax.

TINTING FLOWERS

Tinting flowers is very popular. Commercial growers now color many varieties before they are shipped to the market. The dyes are excellent; it is almost impossible to detect whether the flowers are natural or artificially colored. The array of colors is outstanding. There are several methods used: absorption, dip and rinse, dip and no rinse, and spraying.

First Method: Usually white flowers are used commercially with carnations. The freshly cut flowers are allowed to soften a bit from need of water. The stems are re-cut and immediately placed in the dye solution. As stems absorb the liquid, dye is transported into the petals. It is first noticed in the veins and soon spreads over the entire petal. This usually requires eight to twelve hours at room temperature. A two tone effect is obtained if the flowers do not remain too long in the dye. Do not refrigerate until desired color has been obtained.

Second Method: The second listed is "dip and rinse." When using this type, the blossoms and solution should be at room temperature. The dye may be thinned with a special thinner to obtain the exact tint desired. After dipping flowers in dye solution, rinse in clear water. Should the flowers not dye evenly, it is probably due to the residue of insecticides on the blossoms. If the first blossoms tried do not dye well, rinse the others in clear water and allow to dry for thirty minutes before dipping them into the dye solution. This removes the residue of insecticides which prevents dye from coating evenly.

The following standard makes of ink are excellent for use in tinting where commercial floral dyes are not available:

No. 1. Pink.

Carnations and chrysanthemums—use Sheaffer #32 permanent red ink. Depth of color preferred determines quantity of ink to use, add 1 tablespoon of alum to 1 gallon water.

No. 2, Baby Blue, Medium Blue, and Deep Blue.

Use Waterman or Skrip Washable Ink (blue). Dip lightly for baby blue, dip twice for medium blue. Tint white flower violet for deep blue.

Third Method: The third type of dye is the "dip and no rinse" The flowers and dye should be at room temperature. Each flower should be dyed separately. The flower should be immersed about twenty seconds or more, taken out, and given a slight twirl to remove the excess dye from the ends of the petals. The dye is not rinsed. This dye has a plastic in it which makes the flower last longer.

Fourth Method: The fourth method is spraying colors from pressurized cans. This is a most efficient and economical way of tinting. Colors are natural, soft tones, also a metallic kind is available. Transitional color effects can be gotten by careful use of the spray dye.

All dyed flowers should be allowed to dry for at least an hour or more before they are worn or carried.

If dyes get wet, they will sometimes stain clothing brushed against them. When this happens, inform the cleaning establishment that alcohol will remove the stains from silk, wool, nylon, or rayon. A bleach will remove the stain from linen or cotton.

Chapter VIII

Flower Forms

In geometric design, floral materials, like machinery parts, have definite shapes. They fit together with the same precision as a good mechanical assembly. It is the combination of form that gives interest, imparts vitality and prevents monotony. Variety is the spice of life. The fitting together of forms, one within the other, produces the floral picture. Each shape plays a specific role. The recognition of these shapes will enable one to solve many design problems and prevent others from arising. One type may be used alone in an arrangement or any two or more forms may be combined. The flowers remain individual and are recognized by their own characteristics even though they may be grouped in mass. In geometrical design flowers retain their identity whereas in *Free Form* this identity may be lost.

The four groups of flower types are *line, mass, form* and *filler.*

Line flowers, Figure 21, are generally erect, tall spikes of blossoms with florets blooming along the stem. They give a feeling of length and definitely create linear pattern. *Line* flowers may be placed one next to the other, either back to back, e.g., gladioli forming one single blossom, or

placed end to end continuing a long line. In either case the *line* blossom does not lose its identity. This type flower establishes pattern, sets proportion, and is the framework or skeleton on which to build the design. When measuring *line* flowers with the container, the buds beyond the half-opened blossoms on the upper portion of the stem are not counted in the pattern. Figure 6. Other flower types when combined with *line* flowers are used lower, within the framework set by the line types. Gladiolus, larkspur, stock, delphinium, snapdragon and cattail are examples of *line* flowers.

Mass flowers, Figure 22, have single stems with one solid head. This group of flowers is used "toward" the focal point within the framework of linear materials. When they are used alone in an arrangement the buds or smaller ones are placed to the outer edges and farther apart. As the focal point is approached, larger *mass* flowers are placed closer together to add weight for stability. Never place *mass* type flowers on the same level or plane; this produces a manufactured appearance. Vary the heights and depths so that each one reveals its individual shape; this will give a feeling of depth to an arrangement. The chrysanthemum, dahlia,

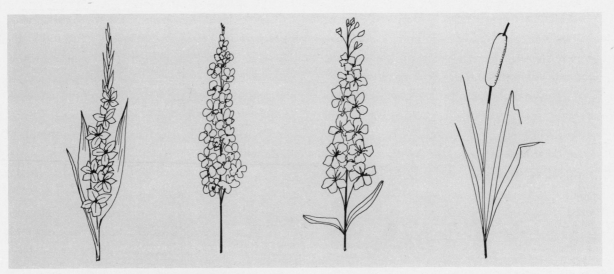

Fig. 21 — *Line flowers.   Gladiolus, delphinium, stock, cattails.*

Fig. 22 — *Mass flowers.   Rose, carnation, zinnia, chrysanthemum.*

peony, rose, carnation and aster are a few examples of *mass* flowers.

Form flowers, Figure 23, have distinctive shapes from which this group derives its name. Their intrinsic value lies in their characteristic form. It is imperative that space be maintained between them if they are to remain individuals. They are sufficient unto themselves; other shapes may detract from them. *Form* flowers are used "at" the focal point. They are superior for this position. Some of them such as bird-of-paradise, anthurium, and calla have strong outlines and can be used as silhouette blossoms on the outer edges of the arrangement. Generally they are more beautiful when used alone.

Filler flowers, Figure 24, may be either bunchy or feathery and are used to "fill in" arrangements. They follow the pattern set by the main blossoms but having less importance are therefore used to the background and low in the arrangement. They add emphasis to the main blossoms. The *bunchy fillers* are generally flowers having many stems with small mass type heads— pompon asters, pompon chrysanthemums and feverfew are included in this group. The *feathery fillers*, gypsophila and caspia or seafoam statice are used like bunchy fillers but give a misty, delicate, feminine effect to an arrangement. It is not considered good taste to use these in stylized masculine designs or with flowers that have severe silhouette value. For example, gypsophila with anthurium.

Reviewing the four types of blossoms it can be said that line flowers are used "*out*", establishing the pattern; mass flowers are used "*toward*" the focal area within this framework; form flowers "*at*" the focal point and filler types used "*behind*" these main blossoms (Figure 25). Again it can be said that any one group or combination of groups may be used in an arrangement. The four types of flowers should be used with foliage which has similar characteristics. The foliage must complement the flowers, e. g., gladioli with linear rather than feathery foliage and sweet peas with fernlike foliage.

By studying several examples it is obvious how each of the four forms *(line, mass, form and filler)* play their part in the design. In Plate 16, the *line* flowers (snapdragons), give the framework, round mass forms (roses and ranunculi), fit within the pattern and form flowers (tulips) are placed within the round forms. Plate 20 is another pattern showing how the flower types conform to this principle. Plate 39, *Parrot Tulips*, is an example of how bells-of-Ireland, *line* flowers, form the linear pattern and the tulips fit into this design. In Plate 60, *Chinoiserie*, the materials, although preserved, are still placed according to their form. *Line* materials, sea plume, reinforced with okra seed pods, establish the "S" curve pattern. Round materials are graduated, beginning with small teasel burrs, then into cardoon, and at the center of interest, larger artichoke blossoms. Lotus seed pods, another round form, add

Fig. 23 — *Form flowers. Orchid, lily, anthurium, strelitzia.*

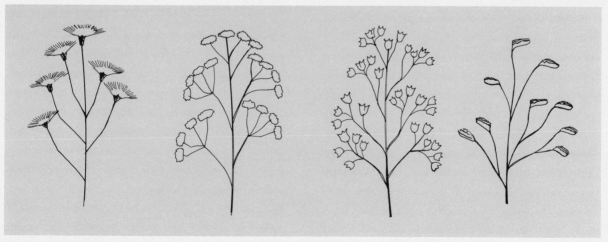

Fig. 24 — *Filler flowers. Pompon aster, feverfew, gypsophila, statice*

227

Fig. 25 — *The four flower forms in combination; line flowers establishing "skeleton"; mass flowers used "toward"; form flowers "at" focal point; filler flowers "behind" main blossoms.*

interest. In Plate 78, *Easter Elegance*, the *line* material, larkspur, gives the oval pattern. Easter lilies are the *form* flowers used which are enhanced by majestic daisies used as *filler*. The grouping of true *filler* type blossoms, feverfew, is used to the lower right and not in its usual position. One can readily see from these illustrations that regardless of the name of the flower or the combination of flowers, it is their shape used in their respective places that produces the floral picture. To readily learn flower arranging (*geometrical design*), one should forget the various names of flowers and concentrate only on the shape and the positions that the shapes take in the design. In the hands of an experienced designer, the shapes may be varied.

Free Form—Interpretive Design is not dictated to by the characteristic shapes of the four groups; the floral material is also used for intrinsic value, color, texture, etc., to meet the demands of the artist. Liberties are taken with blossoms; these are used to produce "abstract" effects and to express ideas. Flowers may lose their identity; as in Plate 1, *Grecian Horse*, where the lilies are inserted one into the other to form the Olympic torch and add dynamic force. The petal shapes repeat the curves of the arched neck of the horse. Also in Plate 33, *Allegorical Tale*, the marigolds are used for color and texture, and for their Guatemalan symbolic meaning. The round form of this flower is not considered. In Plate 10, *Egyptian Pyramid*, strelitzia is used for its silhouette value, reproducing the hieroglyphics and paintings found on the walls of the tombs of the Pharaohs. The strelitzia's etched silhouette form is vital to this design. It is hard to picture any other blossom giving the same effect. In Plate 71, *Surrealism — Space Man*, the flowers and dried materials must be forgotten in their traditional manner. Think of the chrysanthemums as spheres or planets; their petals repeat the curly texture of the dried material. The cockscomb is used for the emotional response of color and not mass that cockscomb would give in traditional designing.

PERMANENT FLOWERS AND FOLIAGE

With the constant use of floral materials we have become accustomed to the various qualities that heretofore were overlooked. These qualities as applied to floral materials, may be described as dried, bleached, painted, tinted, jeweled, artificial, etc. In previous years, due to inexperience, poor technique and inferior quality, these materials were looked upon with disfavor, however, their appreciation has changed with the times. Designers have found that they have great intrinsic value. Beauty in form is recognized, e. g., in Plates 59 and 73, the natural sculptured wood has much intrinsic value. In Plate 32, *Composition — Author's Home*, the permanent arrangement of dried artichoke blossoms and the one strelitzia leaf painted gold, is compatible with its setting. Fresh flowers could not replace the dried material to greater advantage. This is also true in Plate 102, *Autumn Call*, which is an arrangement of both dried and artificial material; it is suitable for a den or lodge.

For various occasions, such as weddings, parties and holidays, the floral materials are readily changed to suit the theme. Appreciation and the great advancement in floral designing is releasing the designer from restriction. Unfortunately, prepared materials used indiscriminately by a novice too often result in a trite, common hodge-podge.

Permanent flowers and foliage have definite appeal; they are timely. They are suitable in the contemporary home, and will blend perfectly or add a note of color where needed. Freedom in the use of permanent materials is illustrated in Plate 5, *Oriental Mysticism*. The story would not be complete without the use of bleached plant forms to express age. Tinted yellow-orange millet seeds represent the Buddhist monks' saffron colored robes; plastic covered wire is a product of today and the golden lotus blossom, sacred to the Oriental, is a symbol of purity — all materials would lose their import without the effect of tinting, bleaching, and painting.

The arrangement in Plate 104, *Winter In The Orient*, was made for an exhibit of Chinese art, 4th to 12th century, at the Houston Museum of Fine Arts. Natural twigs of manzanita are combined with dried seed pods and an accent of cardoon blossoms for the center of interest. The design was inspired by the painting on an urn which predates Japanese Ikebana.

In Plate 1, *Grecian Horse*, the gold allium signifies the golden age of their culture. In Plate 18, *The Three Graces*, the Scotch broom painted white, jeweled with mother-of-pearl, miniature seed pearls, and shells add the perfection to the picture it now has. This ornamentation truly speaks of the elegance of the Rococo period. For simplicity of form, see Plate 2. The dried aspidistra leaves are so perfect in color, form, and accent; the design would suffer without the use of this preserved material in its present form. A very interesting example of using painted form is shown in Plate 66. The beautiful bronze antique Chinese incense burner holds bleached wood which was colored with oxblood and brown shoe polish to obtain the perfect color blend with the tritomas. Fresh flowers alternate with the season, e. g., chrysanthemums, celosia, roses, etc., replace the tritomas. What could be more dramatic than the permanent arrangement, all white and covered in mother-of-pearl, Plate 60.

229

PLATE 104

Winter in the Orient

The stage of development of floral material foretells the season in Japanese design. This arrangement of dried forms was inspired by the painting on the urn which predates Japanese Ikebana.

PLATE 105

Aspidistra

Foliage of strong character sets the pattern and is the featured object. Here variegated aspidistra with two Hahn's golden sansevieria plants and pothos leaves accent the Oriental candle.

Chapter IX

Foliage Types

Foliage is appreciated today for its intrinsic value and interesting characteristics. Floral designers realize its great importance in design. Until recent years foliage was considered just an "extra"; a secondary item of no importance that might be added. But today foliage arrangements are gaining as much prominence as flowers. Their interesting form inspires man, thus creating magnificent decor. Legends and myths evolved from the use of foliage in ceremonial activities. Through the ages man has relied on the various shapes to adorn his person or beautify art, e. g., architecture and sculpture. Greeks used the acanthus leaf as a decorative motif on the Corinthian column. This column is valued today as greatly as it was in ancient times. Laurel signifies peace and authority. Greeks wove the branches into garlands for festive occasions to honor athletes and to decorate pedestals. The Romans borrowed this significant foliage for their celebrations and also used it in their crowns. Nero is often pictured wearing a laurel crown. England has admired ivy for generations. In wedding decorations, it is used for its symbolic meaning of life everlasting. The shamrock is closely associated with Ireland and in America the four-leafed clover signifies good luck. Foliage has intimate appeal.

The range of floral designing has been increased in recent years by the introduction of new plants, improved practices in handling, and availability. Architects and interior designers place much emphasis on the decorative value of green plants which encourages the use of foliage arrangements. Japanese have always cherished foliage in their arrangements; America is becoming aware of its value. Distinction and individuality may be gained by its use.

Foliage of strong character may set the floral pattern as in Plate 105. The beautiful variegated aspidistra forms the asymmetrical design framing the interesting Oriental candle. Hahn's variegated, dwarf sanseviera plants are placed to either side of the candle adding emphasis to the focal area. Large leaves of Pothos (commonly known as devil's ivy) frame the focal point and add weight. In Plates 56, 97 and 98 foliage establishes the pattern; flowers and accessories do enhance the composition and may be changed without interfering with the design. In Plate 38 the agave plant is used at the focal point. The story of floral composition is built around this plant. The flowers are incidental, foliage is featured.

Foliage, like flowers, may be classified according to shape. Fig 26, *Linear* foliage adds strength, vitality, and enhances line in the design. It imparts dignity. Some types are swordlike, e. g., gladiolus, ti, draceana and palm (Molineria) and may curve

Fig. 26

1—*Sansevieria*; 2—*Philodendron (dubia), Monstera*; 3—*Ti—(cordyline terminalis)*; 4—*Lemon (salal)*; 5—*Pothos (devil's ivy)*; 6—*English ivy*; 7—*Caladium*; 8—*Chamaedorea elegans*; 9—*Chamaedorea glaucifolia*; 10—*Fern*; 11—*Eucalyptus*; 12—*Huckleberry*.

232

gracefully, or it may branch freely but still give a linear effect (lycopodium, sea plume), Plates 60 and 67.

A second group of foliage is noted for its *Mass* which gives weight to the composition. Magnolia, broad-leaved philodendron, ficus, Pothos (Scindapsus), dieffenbachia and caladium, are examples. Their broad surfaces form excellent backgrounds for blossoms. A brilliant note of color may be introduced by this foliage, e. g., croton or caladium. In Plate 65. Ficus pandurata (fiddle leaf rubber plant) expresses the lush growth of the jungle and gives needed weight and background. In Plate 47, caladium foliage gives color and background to the arrangement.

A third type of foliage is used for its *Form*. Value is in its distinctive shape or brilliant coloring. Cut-leaf philodendron (P. dubia and Monstera delicosa), anthurium crystallinum, croton, ti and lycopodium are examples. Plate 76 shows a leaf of Monstera of sufficient size to dominate the composition. In Plate 67 the bright color of the foliage and the interesting texture of lycopodium, qualify these plants for this grouping.

The fourth group is of the filler type. Some of the most popular are lemon (salal), huckleberry, plumosus, ligustrum, arborvitae and cherry laurel. Similar to filler flowers, this foliage is used primarily for background and to "tie in" the arrangement. It does not have enough character or importance to establish the pattern but is useful in blending units together.

The combination of flowers with their own foliage can rarely be improved upon. This gives a natural look. In Plate 93 no other foliage would suffice. When this is not feasible, select foliage which complements the flower in line, texture, color, etc. The strong forms of callas, anthurium, strelitzia, etc., require foliage of similar character. Delicate flowers, such as sweet peas, are arrange best with adiantum or other varieties of fern.

The care of foliage is comparable to the care of cut flowers, however, foliage does take more abuse. It must be remembered that foliage is living tissue and needs water to survive. Hard, woody shrubs should have their ends crushed with a hammer to enable them to absorb water. Stems with milky juices must be seared and then submerged under water for several hours to condition. Foliage from the many varieties of ginger, palmetto, canna, caladium, etc., also requires submerging under water for conditioning.

It is wise to grow shrubs in the garden from which to cut needed branches. These plants may be carefully pruned for foliage without damaging their beauty. Visualize the branch in the arrangement before cutting.

SPECIFIC FLOWERS, FOLIAGE, FRUIT

Familiar plant materials vary in each section of the country. What is commonplace to one person is strange or exotic to another; therefore a brief description of some of the unusual ones used in illustrations in this book will be helpful. This list does not include nationally known materials that are self-evident, e. g., roses, carnations, gladioli, and familiar foliage.

ADIANTUM (maidenhair fern) is one of the most beautiful and versatile ferns. It is valued for its use in designs that require delicate foliage of fine quality. Its use has been limited in the Southern States because of its tendency to curl there. It must be soaked under water overnight before using. Since the development and use of floral waxes, it can be used more freely. Floral wax sprayed on the backs of ferns carrying spores prevents shedding.

AGAPANTHUS (A. Africanus) Plate 8. This flower is generally known as lily-of-the-Nile. It is a native of South Africa. It is an excellent potted plant. The flowers are pale blue, violet or white.

ANTHURIUM (A. scherzeriamum) Plates 31 and 65. This plant is native of Central America and is highly prized for its unusual heart-shape flowers and patent leather texture. The colors range from pure white, pale pink through coral to brilliant red. The hybrid varieties have elongated flower points and may be found in variegated colors with green. This is a distinct form flower which has great silhouette value. A. crystallinum is grown for its showy foliage; its heart-shape leaves are of a deep green with mahogany red veins. The surface is covered with soft down (pubescence) which gives a velvet-like texture.

ASPIDISTRA (A. elatior) cast-iron plant. Plates 2, 3, 4, 6, 36 and 105. In Japan this plant is known as "orchid" — its blossoms are at ground level and inconspicuous. Its Oriental meaning is purity. This plant is grown throughout the world for its foliage. The variegated variety will produce white stripes when grown in poor soil. This plant takes much abuse and is a favorite potted plant in buildings which have very little light. To condition the leaves for flower arrangement, roll them in the desired shape and tie with a rubber band or pin securely. The leaves are then soaked under water overnight. For dried use, the fresh leaves may be arranged and as they age, they become a tawny brown color (Plate 97). No glycerine is needed.

AGAVE (A. atrovirens) Century plant, pulque agave, Plate 38. Agave is the name of a large family of succulent plants native to Southern United States and Mexico. It is grown in Mexico as a source of juice from which pulque, a spirituous liquor made by fermenting the juices of maguey (agave), is made. The author grows this as a potted plant. It is uprooted when needed in a flower arrangement and may be used for several months without apparent damage. In Plate 59, the variegated agave leaf was used for approximately six months.

BEAUTY-BERRY (Callicarpa Americana) Plate 80. Callicarpa is Greek for beauty fruit; it is also called French mulberry. It is a deciduous shrub, native of the Southern United States. Its berries are born in compact circular clusters at the node of each joint. This plant is very good to have in the

PLATE 106
Indonesia

Deep red caladium foliage contrasts with the pink tint of the banana blossoms. They not only blend in color but also with the tropical habitat of the Indonesian priest.

yard for birds. Its purplish red fruit is excellent in floral designs.

BEGONIA — numerous varieties. Begonia is excellent as a cut foliage and flower in arrangements. Its texture, color and various forms are valued for this purpose.

BELLS-OF-IRELAND (Molucella laevis) Plates 21 and 39. In the Southern area of the United States this plant is practically a weed when it is allowed to re-seed. The bells are bracts which enclose the small white flowers. It is cut when the lower blossoms have matured, and then defoliated. It may be curved in the desired position and then placed in water or a stiff wire can be inserted up the stem.

234

BOIS D'ARC (Maclura pomifera) also called Osage orange. This fruit is from a tree of the mulberry family and grows practically all over the United States. In the prairie states, it makes a good windbreak and in the years before fencing material was available this tree was grown in hedge rows to form a natural fence. Its chartreuse rough textured fruit may be used for the natural chartreuse coloring or sprayed gold and is most effective in holiday arrangements.

BOUVARDIA (B. Humboldti) Plate 18. This is a greenhouse shrub. The flowers are available at the florists' shops. It is prized for wedding work and flower arrangements where a delicate effect is needed.

CACTI (Opuntia streptacantha) Plate 35. The common prickly pear cactus is excellent for arrangements where a Southwestern appearance is needed. It may be gathered from the fields or the spineless variety grown in the garden for use in arrangements.

CALADIUM — many varieties. Plates 22, 47, 50, 80, 92 and 106. This plant is a favorite potted plant and in Southern areas is grown in gardens for foliage. It is excellent as a cut foliage. One of the finest varieties is White Wing, Plate 50, a strap leaf which is very tough and leathery. It will last from ten days to two weeks in arrangements. Cut the mature leaves, sear the ends of the stems, submerge under water overnight. A clear plastic can be sprayed on the foliage to prevent dehydrating and wilting. The brilliant colors and interesting shapes lend distinction to designing.

CHAMAEDOREA (C. elegans-narrow leaf and C. erumpens — wide leaf). Plate 14. Commercially known as "Jewel" or "Comador" foliage, it is an unusual tropical foliage having the appearance of a palm leaf. It is now imported from Mexico and Central America. It adds new potential to designing. This foliage is becoming very popular in florists' shops, and is available throughout the year. There are two varieties: a wide leaf called "Jade," and a narrow leaf called "Emerald." Narrow fronds can

be formed into severe triangular shapes by trimming, producing a tailored appearance in the design. Ends of the broad leaf frond may be clipped with pinking shears producing the effect of the fish tail palm.

CECROPIA (C. palmata) Plate 13. It is named for King Cecrops of Attica. This dried foliage is from a tropical American tree of the mulberry family. It is commonly called snakewood. The large leaves, 7 to 11 lobes, have a conspicuous white coloring beneath. When dried the top green portion of the leaf turns a tawny brown.

CROTON foliage provides colors of bright yellows, oranges, and reds in the Fall. It is used year round in wedding bouquets, corsages, and flower arrangements. Croton will last longer when sprayed with a clear plastic spray.

DAFFODIL — Plate 93. This foliage does not present any problem. It lasts well in arrangements and is one of the finest of any of the Narcissus family.

DESERT SPOONS (Dasylirion Wheeleri) Plate 65. This plant is also called sotol. The so-called spoons are the base of the leaf that is grown just below ground level — which gives them the creamy white coloring when they are fresh. These spoons are available on the commercial market. Rosettes made by grouping these spoons into a circle form a large magnolia-like blossom. When placed in sequence as in Plate 65 the repetition creates an interesting rhythm.

ECHEVERIA — many varieties. Plates 10 and 68. This succulent plant is excellent in flower arrangements especially in permanent arrangements where no water is supplied. The rosettes make excellent focal points.

EREMURUS (E. bungei) Plate 37. In some areas this flower is called the foxtail lily, or desert candle. Eremurus is from the Greek for lonely tail, probably in reference to the solitary flower cluster. This magnificent perennial herb is dramatic. Its flowers are light yellow through a brilliant orange.

Some varieties have pink and white flowers.

EUCALYPTUS — many varieties. It is available in florists' shops. Spiral eucalyptus is the most popular. It is excellent in contemporary arrangements especially those of Oriental mood. It may be dried by hanging upside down. It retains its gray coloring and responds to glycerine treatment.

GALAX (G. aphylla) is a beautiful bronze color in Autumn. It is native to the Eastern states from Virginia to Georgia. Bunches of this foliage may be purchased from the florists' shops. Its foliage leaf is 4″ to 6″ in width and of very rough texture. It responds nicely to the glycerine treatment. Rosettes may be made of its foliage and used in flower arrangements and wreaths.

GINGER — This large family of plants includes Zingiber, Amomum, Costus, Alpinia, Curcuma and a number of others.

Costus speciosus. Malay, spiral or crape ginger. Plate 59. This particular specie of ginger grows in a spiraling formation. Its value lies in this characteristic. The stem terminates in a rose-pink, cone shaped head from which white blossoms appear. The author grows this plant for its interesting spiral form.

Flame Ginger (Alpinia purpurata) is a common ornamental plant in Hawaii. It is native to the Pacific Islands. The flower spike is from 6-12 inches in length of bright red bracts from which small white flowers emerge. The fresh bracts are brilliant and as they age, they become a deep maroon color.

Tumeric Ginger (Curcuma longa). This beautiful tawny brown blossom is from the herbaceous plant from which the culinary spice turmeric used in curry powder is obtained. Curcuma is the Latinized version for the Arabic word turmeric. This plant is easily grown in Southern climates in the yard and as a potted plant. It blossoms freely. The flower shown in Plate 3 is C. roscoeana, a native of Burma and India.

HOSTA (funkia) many varieties. Plate 8. This is an excellent foliage for flower arrangements. It is versatile. Rosettes made of the graded sizes make excellent centers of interest.

HUCKLEBERRY is a native foliage of the Northwestern United States. It may be purchased in bunches from the florists' shops. This is a filler type foliage.

IVY — 1. English ivy (Hedera helix) is the most popular type. It has been bred by fanciers into many forms. Named varieties are grown as potted plants, as landscape materials, and as foliage for designers. There are both plain green and variegated forms. 2. Pothos or devil's ivy (Scindapsus aureus). Plate 105. This plant grows readily in water or as a potted plant. Its runners as foliage are excellent in design work.

KUMQUAT (Fortunella japonica) Plate 97. This orange-like fruit resembles members of the citrus family and it may be crossed with citrus. The egg-shaped variety is F. crassifolia and the oval shaped fruit is F. margarita. The peel has a high content of sugar and is edible.

LEMON — salal (Gaultheris shallon). Bunches of this foliage may be purchased from the florists' shops. It is an excellent filler foliage. This foliage can easily be covered with show card color or any water base paint. Unusual effects can be obtained by brushing salal with these paints.

LIRIOPE (L. muscari) Plate 8. This is a border plant which produces lavender grape-hyacinth-like flowers. It is excellent in shady areas. In flower arrangements its grassy foliage imparts a natural informal look. Excellent for use in Moribana arrangements.

LYCOPODIUM (L. cernuum) ground pine. Plates 46 and 67. Lycopodium is a club moss. The branching varieties used in these two plates are an import from Hawaii and are available at flower shops. It gives interesting texture and line in arrangements.

MAGNOLIA (M. grandiflora) Plate 69. Magnolia may be purchased in two forms, fresh and prepared. In its prepared form only the leaves are used. They are dyed dark green or red and sold by the pound. Sometimes white enameled magnolia leaves are available. In the Southern states magnolia is sold in bunches freshly cut from trees. For an unusual treatment a solution of half water and half glycerine may be prepared and the fresh, green stems be allowed to absorb this solution for about two weeks. A lovely, glossy, brown foliage will result. It will last in dried arrangements about three years or longer.

MONSTERA DELICIOSA. Frontispiece and Plate 76. This plant resembles the cut leaf philodendron; both have fine qualities for flower arrangements. The flower of this plant is used in the Frontispiece and the leaf with the flower in Plate 76.

ORCHIDS. The family of orchids includes a great number of species, each with a tremendous number of varieties. This plant is the farthest advanced in the evolution of plant life and has adapted itself to all types of climatic conditions.

CYMBIDIUM (terrestial) Plates 18, 54 and 83. This orchid has long lasting qualities, lasting six to eight weeks as a cut flower. Its graceful sprays and unusual colors make it a highly prized blossom.

CYPRIPEDIUM (Paphiopedilum) commonly known as the lady-slipper orchid or moccasin flower. Plate 68. It is tailored in appearance and excellent for design work. This particular family of orchids can be used in a rough textured design recalling a woodland scene or in very fine textured arrangements by using the delicate colored varieties.

PHALAENOPSIS is the beautiful moth orchid from the Philippine Islands. Plates 15, 21, 23 and 55. Its blossoms are white, orchid and pink. Graceful sprays of blossoms create a rhythmic beauty that no other flower can produce.

VANDA (V. caerulea, variety Rothschildiana). Plate 72. Another spray variety of orchid with a wide range of colors; the most prominent one in this group is the blue orchid which is shown in the mobile. It has a much more sturdy appearance than the phalaenopsis.

PALM (Molineria recurvata — miscalled Curculigo latifolia) Plates 31 and 41. This small palm is an excellent potted plant. Its leaves are attached to the main stem of the plant in such a manner that the least breeze keeps them in constant lateral motion. It is superb as a cut foliage where strong character is demanded. In Plate 53 the common palmetto is used. It is native throughout the Southern states. The fronds must be submerged in water to condition them for flower arrangements.

PAPERBUSH (Edgeworthia papyriferia) Plate 71. In Japan this branch is called mitsumata. It was valued in China and Japan for the bark which yields paper-making fiber. Its interesting branching habit of three growths from each joint and the white smooth texture in its dried form makes it interesting to use in designing.

PHILODENDRON — many varieties — same uses as Monstera deliciosa and other ivy.

PINEAPPLE (Ananas comosus) Plates 37, 98 and 74. Dwarf pineapple is a maverick in the Hawaiian Islands. It grows wild on the hillside, no doubt having escaped from cultivation. These tiny pineapples are available as small as 2″ in diameter with long stems. They may be dried and this shape is maintained. The tops can be removed and grown as potted plants. The ones shown in these plates are approximately 3″ in diameter. In Plate 37 graded sizes were used, which were painted white and covered in mother-of-pearl for an interesting textural effect.

RUBBER PLANT (Ficus pandurata and F. elastica) Plates 40 and 65. F. pandurata, fiddle rubber plant, is excellent as background foliage. The stems must be seared and submerged under water overnight to insure their lasting. This leaf may be dried and allowed to curl freely in the process. F. elastica is treated in the same manner.

SANSEVIERIA (S. laurenti and Hahnii) Plates 57 and 105. This plant is commonly called snake plant, mother-in-law's tongue, bow string hemp, etc. Its foliage may be used as in Plate 57 or the dwarf varieties used as in Plate 105. This plant can be used in adverse conditions. To curl sansevieria foliage leaves, either while on the plant or for flower arrangements, deprive the leaves of water until they are pliable, shape into the desired position and pin, then supply the needed water.

SCOTCH BROOM (Cytisus scorpious) Plates 18 and 27. Scotch broom is one of the most fascinating foliages available producing a linear pattern of all plants. Its flexibility enables the designer to manipulate the branches into any desired position. These shapes may be pinned to heavy cardboard and dried. It may be used for several years without any apparent damage.

SMILAX — There are two types of smilax, Southern, and Northern (table or string). Southern smilax is an evergreen vine native to Southern states. It is purchased in bales of 100 running yards and is often used for wedding backgrounds and decorations at Christmas time. It may be bought in small bunches at Christmas time, either natural or painted. Northern table smilax is grown in greenhouses on long strings. It is delicate, light green in color and can be purchased by the string, approximately 3 to 5 feet long. It is excellent for fine table settings.

STRELITZIA, commonly known as bird-of-paradise. Plates 10, 42, 53, 65. It is a member of the banana family, Musacae. It was named for the wife of King George III, Charlotte Sophia of the Mecklenburg-Strelitz family. It is valued by the author for its foliage in addition to its flowers.

S. reginae is a low growing plant with short underground woody stem and no trunk. Its flower, born in a purplish boat-shaped bract, is orange-yellow with a blue tongue. This flower has strong silhouette value. Its outline gives an etched appearance. Interesting uses of the foliage are shown in Plates 74, 81 and 98.

S. Nicolai is the white bird-of-paradise which emerges from a large black boat-shaped bract which is often 15″ in length. It is exotic and spectacular.

Plates 37 and 75 are illustrations of this flower.

TI — (Cordyline terminalis) Plates 67 and 25. This foliage is available at the flower shops in all green or in various rosy hues and a multi-colored form of yellow, green, pink and red combined. This plant is an excellent potted plant and will make rapid growth through summer months when the pot is buried in flower beds. It requires rich soil and much water.

TRITOMA (Kniphofia uvaria) commonly called red hot poker, flaming torch and shooting star. Plates 52 and 61. This flower may be obtained in colors of pale chartreuse-yellow to the brilliant orange-reds. It is fascinating in design, not only for its brilliant coloring but because it continues to vary its position as it ages in water. To hold these flowers in the preferred place, insert a wire in the hollow center of the stem.

UMBRELLA PLANT (Cyperus alternifolius) Plate 8. This plant is excellent in the garden or as a potted plant, supplying an interesting foliage for flower arranging. It is best to submerge in water overnight to condition for flower arrangements.

Chapter X

Mechanical Aids

All who work with them soon discover that the flowers are not as cooperative as might be desired. Sometimes they refuse to stay in place, or they curve the wrong way, or they push each other around when your back is turned. Good designers do not leave stability of a design to chance. They anchor each flower and each foliage stem as securely as possible. This phase of designing is not art, it is craftsmanship and must be mastered.

The mechanical construction (such as wiring, securing frogs, etc.) should be concealed as much as possible yet not to the detriment of the design. In flower shows, points are discounted for construction being evident. However, in Japanese arrangements the kubari cannot be concealed in many cases. The correct view of an Oriental design is eye level; the mechanics then would not show (Plate 6). Tall clear glass containers present a problem in some cases; the stems may become a part of the design and clearly show or the flowers may be arranged within the container thus hiding the frog as in Plates 34 and 52.

A flower stem holder, commonly called a "frog," is any object that is used to hold stems securely in position. There is no limit to the types of materials to serve this purpose. In addition to the well known pin/needle point frog or chicken wire, hardware cloth, strips of sheet lead, sand, waste flower stems, blocks of "non-spillable water," and shedded plastic foam all are used with varying success as frogs. The selection depends on the type bowl or vase, the kind of flowers, and the manner in which the arrangement is being used. Another important factor in determining the type of frog is whether or not the arrangement is Oriental or Occidental. For example, the kubari (Oriental) in the arrangement in Plate 2 is vital to the beauty of this design because there is the least evidence of a frog. Trying to hide this part of mechanics would be detrimental to the final picture. In America, arrangements are viewed from all levels.

Frogs	Containers	Security Materials
1. Pin/needle point	open bowls	floral clay
2. Chicken wire (1″ or 2″ mesh)	vases and urns	use wire clamps (hog rings) on inexpensive containers
3. Hardware cloth	vases and urns	roll or crimp
4. Cage-plastic or wire	open bowls	floral clay
5. Non-spillable water: Oasis Sno-pak	all types	as directed, Meyer tape
6. Expanded rock: Vermiculite Terra-lite Tufflite	vase only	fill before adding water
7. Cut foliage	not recommended — sours water	
8. Glass with holes	best to use as a pencil holder and not as a frog	
9. Japanese frogs	see Japanese methods	

239

The most common type frog is the needle point holder. It is advisable to purchase those that have brass points only and that are flat on the bottom. Brass will not rust; inexpensive frogs have steel points that soon rust and ruin the container. Flat bases on the frogs are important in securing the frog to the container.

One important bit of advice: when you purchase a container, buy the right frog at the same time and secure it to the container permanently. Have the joy of these two items being ready when you need them. Floral clay will hold for years without needing to be removed.

Securing Frogs

Learning to secure frogs and flowers is one of the most valuable lessons in design. Some people like to call these methods "tricks of the trade." Actually, only common sense and ingenuity are needed to accomplish the job. An arrangement cannot be transported if the frog is wobbly or likely to slip when the stems are being inserted. This step in mechanics is a "must" and should be accomplished before trying to complete any floral work. Designers have learned through practice their preference as to the frog that serves them best.

The following methods will aid greatly in determining one's selection of frogs:

1. Pin or Needle Holders: To fasten a pin frog securely, a piece of floral clay is worked with the fingers until it is soft and pliable, then it is rolled between palms of the hands or on a flat surface until it is worked into a roll. This roll is placed on the bottom of the frog around the outer edge, forming a complete circle (both frog and container must be *DRY*), Figure 27. Then the frog is pressed firmly on the bottom of container with a twisting motion; the clay flattens out, forming a slight suction cup which holds the frog securely. Use a hot-plate pad over the points to prevent injury to the hand. If difficulty is experienced in securing the frog by this method, the bottom of frog and surface of container may be rubbed with clay before applying the circle

of clay. Some brands of floral clay should not be used in silver containers because they leave a stain that cannot be removed; check on the carton for this information.

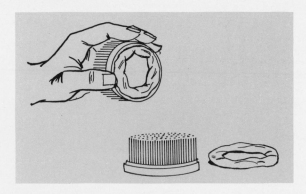

Fig. 27 — *Applying a circle of floral clay to hold the pin frog securely.*

2. Chicken Wire: Excellent frogs may be made of 1″ or 2″ mesh chicken wire. The 1″ mesh chicken wire 12″ wide is the most convenient size. A strip may be cut long enough to brace against the sides of the container, then force it within a short distance of the bottom of the container, and fold the rest of it across the top or near the top. Thus the stems of the flowers will go through two thicknesses of wire — one near the bottom of container and the other near the top. It must be fastened securely to the container as follows:

Chicken wire can be secured to papier-maché containers — or to reasonably priced glass containers with wire clamps (hog rings) which are clamped to the edges with a pair of pliers made especially for this work (Figure 28). These clamps may be purchased from a farm supply store or an automobile accessory shop.

For a low bowl, a small piece of chicken wire may be rolled into a ball, wired onto a rubber suction cup, and placed in bottom of container (Figure 29). The container and suction cup should be wet before securing cup to bottom. These suction cups may be purchased from an automobile accessory shop. They have a coat hanger hook on them.

When securing chicken wire in a bowl or tall vase where suction cups will not fit, another piece

Fig. 28 — *Wire clamps (hog rings) applied with special pliers (hog ringer) holds chicken wire to a container.*

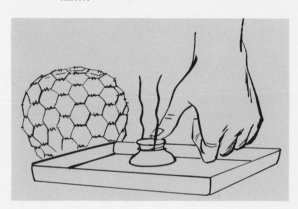

Fig. 29 — *A ball of chicken wire held to a low open bowl with a suction cup.*

of wire may be used to tie it around the top edge of container. This tying wire should be floral taped or inserted in cellophane straws so that it will not rust the container. A tape (Meyers brand) is especially made for this purpose.

For clear glass containers the chicken wire may be secured to cover the mouth of container. Tape two pieces of heavy florist wire (Gauge #16 or #18) with green floral tape and make a "saddle" of the two taped wires across the opening of container, clamping onto the sides. Shape chicken wire to conform to opening and secure to the "saddle." The stems of the flowers will go through and form

a part of the floral pattern. Figure 30.

3. *Hardware Cloth* is another type wire mesh

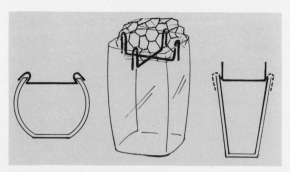

Fig. 30 — *Frogs of chicken wire for clear glass containers can be secured to opening with a "saddle" using heavy gauge taped wire.*

that may be used. It is cut the width of the top of container and is crimped over the edge. This wire is very stiff, cumbersome and cannot be manipulated as easily as chicken wire.

Candles may be secured into needle point holders by tying a circle of hardware cloth (approximately 2″ wide) around the candles and extending beyond candles ½″. Figure 31.

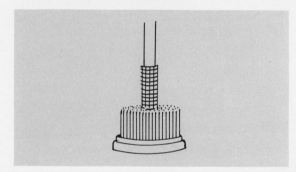

Fig. 31 — *A candle holder of hardware cloth to be used on pin frogs.*

4. *Cage Type* frogs, either plastic or wire, may be secured with floral clay or suction cups. These are not as versatile as pin frogs but are useful after much practice, however, their scope of utility is limited.

5. The blocks of material called *"Non-Spillable Water"* are excellent as frogs. There are two on the market, Oasis and Sno-pak. This material opens new vistas in floral design. Such objects as candle-

241

sticks, narrow neck containers, and arrangements on mirrors using no container, can now be used for flower arrangements. In Plate 21, "Line of Beauty," a block of Oasis is used on a candlestick. A cup or dish of foil was made for the block to prevent leaking, then wrapped with chicken wire to give strength and security. A dowel pin was placed in the candleholder and the reinforced block slipped over it. The flowers were all short stemmed and inserted into this frog. "Non-spillable water" blocks are excellent for very shallow bowls or in arrangements when no conventional bowl or vase is used. In Plates 49, 50, 73 and 80, this material is used to great advantage.

6. *Expanded Rock* (e.g., Vermiculite or Terralite, two commercial brands), and Tufflite filler, another commercial item, are excellent to fill containers and use for frogs. Containers are filled with these materials first and then they are filled with water. In Plates 42 and 64, Tufflite is used as the frog.

7. Filling the container with *Foliage* is not recommended as a holder. The water sours quickly and the life of the flowers is greatly shortened.

8. *Molded Glass* with holes is a very poor frog. It is difficult to secure and does not allow any freedom in design. It is best used as a pencil holder.

9. *Japanese Methods:* Japanese methods are useful in many instances for special effects. Those wishing to follow strictly Oriental custom of Ikebana will naturally use the accepted ways. The author finds Japanese methods excellent for many Free Form designs as in Plates 2, 3, 4 and 6 where the kubari is employed.

1. A kubari is either a "Y" shaped branch or a twig that has been split in two pieces and tied at one end forming a "V". This is fit across the opening of the container. Flowers and foliage are placed in the crotch of this holder and are held in place with a cross-piece of twig called a "komi." This is an excellent way of holding the nemoto in position. The stems of

the materials are cut on a slant to press against the sides of the container and extend through the kubari, as in Plate 6. Oriental containers have rims inside of the opening to prevent the kubari from slipping. Figure 32.

2. A second method of holding stems in place is by splitting the stem up for 1" or 2" and inserting another stem into the split, perpendicular to the main stem. Tie the cross piece in place if it is loose. The inserted cross piece will hold the flower or branch very steady. Figure 33.

3. To hold long stems in a cylindrical vase, a bend is made up the stem (it may break, but must not sever) approximately the diameter of the container, and wedged across the bottom of the container. The now "L" shaped stem holds the upright blossom in place. Figure 34.

4. Japanese knots for tying stems are serviceable. A loop is made and held onto the stems, then with the long end of the cord, bind the loop and the ends of the stems together leaving the loop free above this circling cord. This tying end is run through the loop. The short end (which formed the loop) is pulled downward tightly which binds the cord securely. Figure 35.

MISCELLANEOUS AIDS

Wire-types:

1. Spool wire: ¼ lb. to stick, useful for making garlands and for corsage work.
2. Cut wire: 18" or 24" lengths. Useful gauges #18, #19, #20 for flower arment, #24 and #28 for corsage work and tying stems.

Uses of Wire:

1. Curve a stem into the position or line desired, e.g., Plate 58, *Contemporary Ikenobo.*
2. Straighten a crooked stem.
3. Strengthen a weak stem and prevent drooping.

Fig. 32 — *A kubari made of a "Y" shaped branch. Stems are held in place with a cross-piece — komi.*

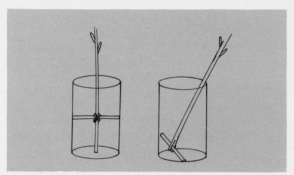

Fig. 33 — *A twig is inserted in a split section of stem and is used as a brace.*

Fig. 34 — *A stem is broken in to "L" shape to hold upright blossom in place.*

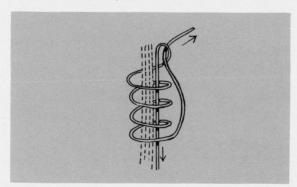

Fig. 35 — *A Japanese knot for tying stems.*

4. Group small stemmed flowers into mass effects.

5. Stabilize the arrangement — some flowers tend to vary their position, e.g., tritomas, tulips.

6. Construct a composite flower, e.g., glamellias, galax and ivy rosettes, etc.

7. Reduce weight in corsages by replacing stems.

Picks are purchased in bundles of 2½", 3", 4" and 6" lengths. They are useful to:

1. Provide a firm wooden stem to insert into the foundation.

2. Provide extra stem lengths.

3. Provide stems for dried or artificial material.

4. Provide stems for fruit

Greening Pins are used for applying greens to flat surfaces, e.g., foliage on a wreath.

Bank Pins #24 are excellent for holding stems together as in Plates 36 and 42.

MECHANICAL PROBLEMS

The use of wire and picks, like the use of frogs, is a matter of craftsmanship. There are certain practices which may be learned by experience and observation. Flowers must also be conditioned to conform to one's desires. The following suggestions may help solve many mechanical problems:

1. Flowers must be removed from the refrigerator several hours before stems are to be curved. Flowers that have been cut for a day or so are more flexible than freshly cut flowers. They can be shaped into pleasing curves by flexing the stems gently with the fingers. Stems may be made more flexible by massaging them gently. Both flower stems and foliage may be curved in this manner.

2. When a gladiolus stem does not bend correctly, the stem tissue may be split lengthwise by placing the gladiolus on the table and pressing the fingers or palm downward. (Figure 36). This should be done carefully so that the stem does not

243

break crosswise, or the flow of water will be impeded.

3. To straighten succulent stems of callas, tritomas and tulips, roll them in newspapers and place in water for several hours before using.

4. When using a low container with shallow

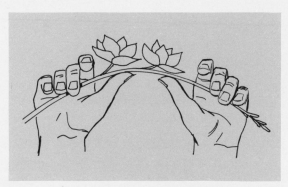

Fig. 36 — *To flex gladiolus stems by applying pressure gently to split stems lengthwise.*

water, it is important to cut flower stems with a long slant and to place cuts downward so the stems can take up water. A cut in any other direction may not be covered by water. In securing slanting stems to pin frogs, the fingers are never used to press stems in place; another stem may be used to do the pressing to prevent injury (Figure 37).

5. When working with low containers, the frog is placed at the point where the center of interest, or focal point, originates. This is done regardless of the type of frog used. If the arrangement is to have a high left and a low right, the frog is placed left of center. In a symmetrical ar-

Fig. 37 — *Place slanting cut face downward toward water. Use another stem for pressing.*

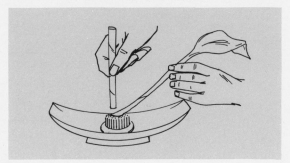

rangement the frog is centered in the container.

6. If a small stemmed flower will not stick in a pin frog, a small piece of gladiolus stem (or other fleshy stem) may be cut approximately ½″ in length and the small stem forced completely through this cut section, then onto the frog (Figure 38). If the small stem is too soft to force through the larger stem, a nail or pick may be used to punch a pilot hole in the larger stem.

7. A piece of plastic foam placed on a pin frog is helpful when securing dried materials such as cattails, grasses, or Christmas ornaments. If dried materials are used in combination with fresh flowers in an arrangement, the plastic foam may

Fig. 38 — *Use a cross section of a fleshy stem in which to insert small stems.*

be placed on the back side of the pin frog and the fresh flowers arranged first; then the dried materials or ornaments may be inserted in the plastic foam.

8. To wire hollow stem flowers, e.g., daffodils, wire may be inserted up the stem into the neck of blossom. It will curve easily and the mechanics will not show.

9. When stems are a major feature in design and mechanics would ruin the effect, if visible, e.g., callas in Plates 58, 62 and 63, the following procedure is employed: First, stems are wilted by leaving them out of water for several hours or until softened. Wires are then inserted up the full length of the stems and shaped to desired position.

10. One line flower may be placed next to another line flower to continue the length of the

blossoms; they are positioned first, and then a rather stiff wire (gauge #18 or #19) is run horizontally through the stems (See Figure 39). The wire is cut close to the stem. This will keep them from coming apart. There is no need to bind the two stems with wire.

11. A Christmas ornament may be held in position by inserting a wire into a cork and then placing the cork into the opening of the ornament. This wire serves as a stem.

Fig. 39 — *Insert a heavy wire through parallel stems to fasten securely.*

12. To wire a weak stem, a wire longer than the stem is used. A last twist is made around the end of stem and the extra portion is bent upward to act as an arm or brace.

13. A similar brace may be used on a strong stem that does not need wiring but does need bracing, such as roses, carnations, etc., in a chicken-wire frog. The wire is secured around the base of the stem and then its ends are turned upward. This gives a U-shaped brace and aids in holding flowers in position (Figure 40).

14. Fleshy-stemmed flowers, such as callas, tritomas and gladioli, may be fastened to chicken-wire frogs by pushing stems downward over the bottom layer of wire, thus cutting up into the stems.

15. Another way of keeping fleshy stemmed flowers in position, when they insist on turning in

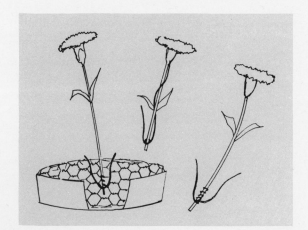

Fig. 40 — *Leave the surplus wire on end of stem and turn upward to hold flower in place. Or apply extension wire to stem and turn both ends upward to hold flower in place.*

a circular motion, is to insert a heavy wire through the top layer of the chicken-wire frog, piercing the stems of the flowers near top of container. This horizontal wire will serve as a brace. There is no need to twist this wire down into the chicken-wire frog or bend it over the edge of the container.

16. When working with roses, carnations or other small-stemmed flowers whose stems will not stay in the pin frog, the flowers may be grouped together in the desired position and ends secured by binding wire around them (Figure 41). The group is then placed on the frog. A rubber band or raffia may also be used to hold a grouping of stems.

Fig. 41 — *Bind small stems together to be inserted on pin frog.*

17. To firmly secure tall stems or fleshy stems on pin frogs, tightly bind the end of the stem with #28 gauge wire and insert on pins. This method enables the designer to give strength to the stem. The stem ends will not be splintered.

18. When extra height is needed in an arrangement, stems may be inserted in orchid tubes, then tied to sticks or other stems and placed in position (Figure 42).

19. Frogs cannot be used in the bottom of clear, crystal containers where the stems of flowers play an important part in the design. In such cases,

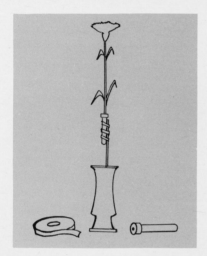

Fig. 42 — *Use water picks or discarded orchid tubes tied to a stick to lengthen short stems.*

a narrow piece of sheet lead may be used, which may be bought from plumbing suppliers. It is bound around the flower stems and then folded over the top edge of container (Figure 43). A flower or some foliage is then placed at this point to cover the frog.

20. The problem of hiding stems and frogs in clear, crystal containers may also be solved by adding dye to the water, or by lining the container with crushed cellophane before placing the frog in position.

21. A pair of tongs is convenient for placing an arrangement in a deep, clear glass container such as a brandy snifter (Figure 44). Because of the narrow openings, arrangements for containers

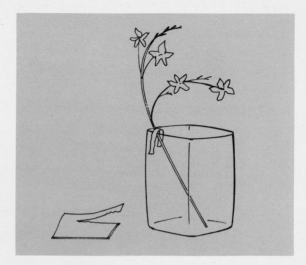

Fig. 43 — *Strips of sheet lead are excellent ties to hold stems at upper edge of clear glass containers.*

Fig. 44 — *Tongs are used to lower main portion of flower arrangement in narrow mouth containers.*

Fig. 45 — *Reflexing tulip or rose petals.*

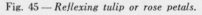

of this type are often made up on the outside. Have the container near the arrangement while it is being made so that the arrangement can be visualized in the container and the size and placement of the blossoms judged correctly.

22. When designing an arrangement on a mirror or glass wall use a block of "non-spillable water" reinforced with chicken wire for a container and secure this to the mirror with a suction cup. Dampen the cup with glycerine and not with water; the glycerine does not dry.

23. To secure a wreath on a mirror or glass door use a suction cup.

24. Reflexing petals: Place the thumb against the center of a petal or calyx, then with the index and middle finger gently pull back the petal or calyx causing it to reverse. This increases the size of a flower such as a rose or tulip. With carnations, the reflexed calyx allows the petals more freedom, thus producing a larger flower (Fig. 45).

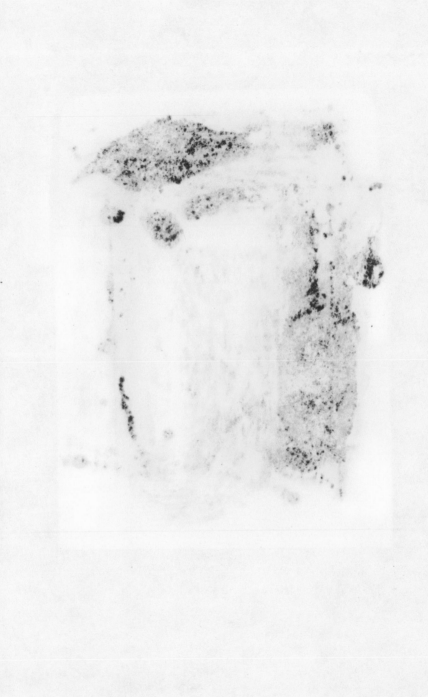